Jump Start Your Career
in Technology & IT
in about 100 Pages

Table of Contents

Let's Start !

Acknowledgements

My thanks to all the people who contributed to this book. The Syncfusion team conceived the idea for this book and then made it happen—Hillary Bowling, Graham High, and Tres Watkins. The lead technical editor, Chris Lee, thoroughly reviewed the book's organization, code quality, and calculation accuracy. Several of my colleagues at Microsoft acted as technical and editorial reviewers, and provided many helpful suggestions for improving the book in areas such as overall correctness, coding style, readability, and implementation alternatives—many thanks to Jamilu Abubakar, Todd Bello, Cyrus Cousins, Marciano Moreno Diaz Covarrubias, Suraj Jain, Tomasz Kaminski, Sonja Knoll, Rick Lewis, Chen Li, Tom Minka, Tameem Ansari Mohammed, Delbert Murphy, Robert Musson, Paul Roy Owino, Sayan Pathak, David Raskino, Robert Rounthwaite, Zhefu Shi, Alisson Sol, Gopal Srinivasa, and Liang Xie.

Chapter 1 *k*-Means Clustering

Introduction

Data clustering is the process of placing data items into groups so that similar items are in the same group (cluster) and dissimilar items are in different groups. After a data set has been clustered, it can be examined to find interesting patterns. For example, a data set of sales transactions might be clustered and then inspected to see if there are differences between the shopping patterns of men and women.

There are many different clustering algorithms. One of the most common is called the *k*-means algorithm. A good way to gain an understanding of the *k*-means algorithm is to examine the screenshot of the demo program shown in **Figure 1-a**. The demo program groups a data set of 10 items into three clusters. Each data item represents the height (in inches) and weight (in kilograms) of a person.

The data set was artificially constructed so that the items clearly fall into three distinct clusters. But even with only 10 simple data items that have only two values each, it is not immediately obvious which data items are similar:

```
(73.0, 72.6)
(61.0, 54.4)
(67.0, 99.9)
(68.0, 97.3)
(62.0, 59.0)
(75.0, 81.6)
(74.0, 77.1)
(66.0, 97.3)
(68.0, 93.3)
(61.0, 59.0)
```

However, after *k*-means clustering, it is clear that there are three distinct groups that might be labeled "medium-height and heavy", "tall and medium-weight", and "short and light":

```
(67.0, 99.9)
(68.0, 97.3)
(66.0, 97.3)
(68.0, 93.3)

(73.0, 72.6)
(75.0, 81.6)
(74.0, 77.1)

(61.0, 54.4)
(62.0, 59.0)
(61.0, 59.0)
```

The *k*-means algorithm works only with strictly numeric data. Each data item in the demo has two numeric components (height and weight), but *k*-means can handle data items with any number of values, for example, (73.0, 72.6, 98.6), where the third value is body temperature.

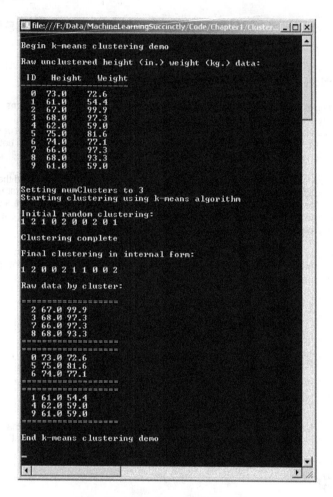

```
file:///F:/Data/MachineLearningSuccinctly/Code/Chapter1/Cluster...    _ □ ×

Begin k-means clustering demo

Raw unclustered height (in.) weight (kg.) data:
 ID    Height    Weight

  0    73.0      72.6
  1    61.0      54.4
  2    67.0      99.9
  3    68.0      97.3
  4    62.0      59.0
  5    75.0      81.6
  6    74.0      77.1
  7    66.0      97.3
  8    68.0      93.3
  9    61.0      59.0


Setting numClusters to 3
Starting clustering using k-means algorithm

Initial random clustering:
1 2 1 0 2 0 0 2 0 1

Clustering complete

Final clustering in internal form:

1 2 0 0 2 1 1 0 0 2

Raw data by cluster:

====================
  2 67.0 99.9
  3 68.0 97.3
  7 66.0 97.3
  8 68.0 93.3
====================
  0 73.0 72.6
  5 75.0 81.6
  6 74.0 77.1
====================
  1 61.0 54.4
  4 62.0 59.0
  9 61.0 59.0
====================

End k-means clustering demo

_
```

Figure 1-a: The k-Means Algorithm in Action

Notice that in the demo program, the number of clusters (the *k* in *k*-means) was set to 3. Most clustering algorithms, including *k*-means, require that the user specify the number of clusters, as opposed to the program automatically finding an optimal number of clusters. The *k*-means algorithm is an example of what is called an unsupervised machine learning technique because the algorithm works directly on the entire data set, without any special training items (with cluster membership pre-specified) required.

The demo program initially assigns each data tuple randomly to one of the three cluster IDs. After the clustering process finished, the demo displays the resulting clustering: { 1, 2, 0, 0, 2, 1, 1, 0, 0, 2 }, which means data item 0 is assigned to cluster 1, data item 1 is assigned to cluster 2, data item 2 is assigned to cluster 0, data item 3 is assigned to cluster 0, and so on.

Understanding the *k*-Means Algorithm

A naive approach to clustering numeric data would be to examine all possible groupings of the source data set and then determine which of those groupings is best. There are two problems with this approach. First, the number of possible groupings of a data set grows astronomically large, very quickly. For example, the number of ways to cluster $n = 50$ into $k = 3$ groups is:

119,649,664,052,358,811,373,730

Even if you could somehow examine one billion groupings (also called partitions) per second, it would take you well over three million years of computing time to analyze all possibilities. The second problem with this approach is that there are several ways to define exactly what is meant by the best clustering of a data set.

There are many variations of the *k*-means algorithm. The basic *k*-means algorithm, sometimes called Lloyd's algorithm, is remarkably simple. Expressed in high-level pseudo-code, *k*-means clustering is:

```
randomly assign all data items to a cluster
loop until no change in cluster assignments
  compute centroids for each cluster
  reassign each data item to cluster of closest centroid
end
```

Even though the pseudo-code is very short and simple, *k*-means is somewhat subtle and best explained using pictures. The left-hand image in **Figure 1-b** is a graph of the 10 height-weight data items in the demo program. Notice an optimal clustering is quite obvious. The right image in the figure shows one possible random initial clustering of the data, where color (red, yellow, green) indicates cluster membership.

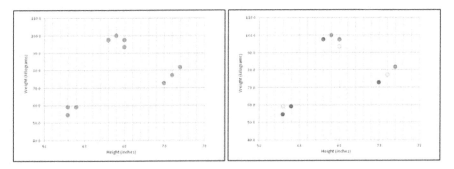

Figure 1-b: k-Means Problem and Cluster Initialization

After initializing cluster assignments, the centroids of each cluster are computed as shown in the left-hand graph in **Figure 1-c**. The three large dots are centroids. The centroid of the data items in a cluster is essentially an average item. For example, you can see that the four data items assigned to the red cluster are slightly to the left, and slightly below, the center of all the data points.

There are several other clustering algorithms that are similar to the k-means algorithm but use a different definition of a centroid item. This is why the k-means is named "k-means" rather than "k-centroids."

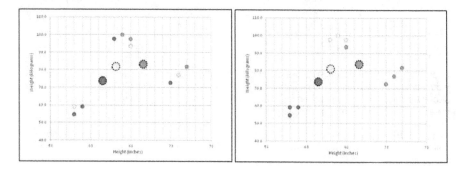

Figure 1-c: Compute Centroids and Reassign Clusters

After the centroids of each cluster are computed, the k-means algorithm scans each data item and reassigns each to the cluster that is associated with the closet centroid, as shown in the right-hand graph in **Figure 1-c**. For example, the three data points in the lower left part of the graph are clearly closest to the red centroid, so those three items are assigned to the red cluster.

The k-means algorithm continues iterating the update-centroids and update-clustering process as shown in **Figure 1-d**. In general, the k-means algorithm will quickly reach a state where there are no changes to cluster assignments, as shown in the right-hand graph in **Figure 1-d**.

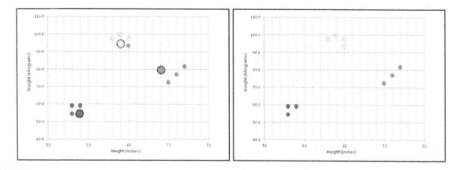

Figure 1-d: Update-Centroids and Update-Clustering Until No Change

The preceding explanation of the *k*-means algorithm leaves out some important details. For example, just how are data items initially assigned to clusters? Exactly what does it mean for a cluster centroid to be closest to a data item? Is there any guarantee that the update-centroids, update-clustering loop will exit?

Demo Program Overall Structure

To create the demo, I launched Visual Studio and selected the new C# console application template. The demo has no significant .NET version dependencies, so any version of Visual Studio should work.

After the template code loaded into the editor, I removed all using statements at the top of the source code, except for the single reference to the top-level System namespace. In the Solution Explorer window, I renamed the Program.cs file to the more descriptive ClusterProgram.cs, and Visual Studio automatically renamed class Program to ClusterProgram.

The overall structure of the demo program, with a few minor edits to save space, is presented in **Listing 1-a**. Note that in order to keep the size of the example code small, and the main ideas as clear as possible, the demo programs violate typical coding style guidelines and omit error checking that would normally be used in production code. The demo program class has three static helper methods. Method ShowData displays the raw source data items.

```
using System;
namespace ClusterNumeric
{
  class ClusterProgram
  {
    static void Main(string[] args)
    {
      Console.WriteLine("\nBegin k-means clustering demo\n");

      double[][] rawData = new double[10][];
      rawData[0] = new double[] { 73, 72.6 };
      rawData[1] = new double[] { 61, 54.4 };
      // etc.
      rawData[9] = new double[] { 61, 59.0 };

      Console.WriteLine("Raw unclustered data:\n");
      Console.WriteLine(" ID    Height (in.)   Weight (kg.)");
      Console.WriteLine("-------------------------------------");
      ShowData(rawData, 1, true, true);

      int numClusters = 3;
      Console.WriteLine("\nSetting numClusters to " + numClusters);

      Console.WriteLine("\nStarting clustering using k-means algorithm");
      Clusterer c = new Clusterer(numClusters);
      int[] clustering = c.Cluster(rawData);
      Console.WriteLine("Clustering complete\n");

      Console.WriteLine("Final clustering in internal form:\n");
      ShowVector(clustering, true);

      Console.WriteLine("Raw data by cluster:\n");
```

```
      ShowClustered(rawData, clustering, numClusters, 1);

      Console.WriteLine("\nEnd k-means clustering demo\n");
      Console.ReadLine();
    }

    static void ShowData(double[][] data, int decimals, bool indices,
      bool newLine) { . . }
    static void ShowVector(int[] vector, bool newLine) { . . }
    static void ShowClustered(double[][] data, int[] clustering,
      int numClusters, int decimals) { . . }
  }

  public class Clusterer { . . }

} // ns
```

Listing 1-a: k-Means Demo Program Structure

Helper ShowVector displays the internal clustering representation, and method ShowClustered displays the source data after it has been clustered, grouped by cluster.

All the clustering logic is contained in a single program-defined class named Clusterer. All the program logic is contained in the Main method. The Main method begins by setting up 10 hard-coded, height-weight data items in an array-of-arrays style matrix:

```
static void Main(string[] args)
{
  Console.WriteLine("\nBegin k-means clustering demo\n");
  double[][] rawData = new double[10][];
  rawData[0] = new double[] { 73, 72.6 };
. . .
```

In a non-demo scenario, you would likely have data stored in a text file, and would load the data into memory using a helper function, as described in the next section. The Main method displays the raw data like so:

```
Console.WriteLine("Raw unclustered data:\n");
Console.WriteLine(" ID   Height (in.)   Weight (kg.)");
Console.WriteLine("-------------------------------------");
ShowData(rawData, 1, true, true);
```

The four arguments to method ShowData are the matrix of type double to display, the number of decimals to display for each value, a Boolean flag to display indices or not, and a Boolean flag to print a final new line or not. Method ShowData is defined in **Listing 1-b**.

```
static void ShowData(double[][] data, int decimals, bool indices, bool newLine)
{
  for (int i = 0; i < data.Length; ++i)
  {
    if (indices == true)
      Console.Write(i.ToString().PadLeft(3) + "  ");
    for (int j = 0; j < data[i].Length; ++j)
```

```
    {
        double v = data[i][j];
        Console.Write(v.ToString("F" + decimals) + "    ");
    }
    Console.WriteLine("");
    }
    if (newLine == true)
        Console.WriteLine("");
}
```

Listing 1-b: Displaying the Raw Data

One of many alternatives to consider is to pass to method ShowData an additional string array parameter named something like "header" that contains column names, and then use that information to display column headers.

In method Main, the calling interface to the clustering routine is very simple:

```
int numClusters = 3;
Console.WriteLine("\nSetting numClusters to " + numClusters);
Console.WriteLine("\nStarting clustering using k-means algorithm");
Clusterer c = new Clusterer(numClusters);
int[] clustering = c.Cluster(rawData);
Console.WriteLine("Clustering complete\n");
```

The program-defined Clusterer constructor accepts a single argument, which is the number of clusters to assign the data items to. The Cluster method accepts a matrix of data items and returns the resulting clustering in the form of an integer array, where the array index value is the index of a data item, and the array cell value is a cluster ID. In the screenshot in **Figure 1-a**, the return array has the following values:

{ 1, 2, 0, 0, 2, 1, 0, 0, 2 }

This means data item [0], which is (73.0, 72.6), is assigned to cluster 1, data [1] is assigned to cluster 2, data [2] is assigned to cluster 0, data [3] is assigned to cluster 0, and so on.

The Main method finishes by displaying the clustering, and displaying the source data grouped by cluster ID:

```
. . .
    Console.WriteLine("Final clustering in internal form: \n");
    ShowVector(clustering, true);

    Console.WriteLine("Raw data by cluster:\n");
    ShowClustered(rawData, clustering, numClusters, 1);

    Console.WriteLine("\nEnd k-means clustering demo\n");
    Console.ReadLine();
}
```

Helper method ShowVector is defined:

```
static void ShowVector(int[] vector, bool newLine)
```

```
{
  for (int i = 0; i < vector.Length; ++i)
    Console.Write(vector[i] + " ");
  if (newLine == true) Console.WriteLine("\n");
}
```

An alternative to relying on a static helper method to display the clustering result is to define a class ToString method along the lines of:

```
Console.WriteLine(c.ToString()); // display clustering[]
```

Helper method ShowClustered displays the source data in clustered form and is presented in **Listing 1-c**. Method ShowClustered makes multiple passes through the data set that has been clustered. A more efficient, but significantly more complicated alternative, is to define a local data structure, such as an array of List objects, and then make a first, single pass through the data, storing the clusterIDs associated with each data item. Then a second, single pass through the data structure could print the data in clustered form.

```
static void ShowClustered(double[][] data, int[] clustering, int numClusters,
  int decimals)
{
  for (int k = 0; k < numClusters; ++k)
  {
    Console.WriteLine("====================");
    for (int i = 0; i < data.Length; ++i)
    {
      int clusterID = clustering[i];
      if (clusterID != k) continue;
      Console.Write(i.ToString().PadLeft(3) + " ");
      for (int j = 0; j < data[i].Length; ++j)
      {
        double v = data[i][j];
        Console.Write(v.ToString("F" + decimals) + " ");
      }
      Console.WriteLine("");
    }
    Console.WriteLine("====================");
  } // k
}
```

Listing 1-c: Displaying the Data in Clustered Form

An alternative to using a static method to display the clustered data is to implement a class member ToString method to do so.

Loading Data from a Text File

In non-demo scenarios, the data to be clustered is usually stored in a text file. For example, suppose the 10 data items in the demo program were stored in a comma-delimited text file, without a header line, named HeightWeight.txt like so:

```
73.0,72.6
61.0,54.4
. . .
61.0,59.0
```

One possible implementation of a LoadData method is presented in **Listing 1-d**. As defined, method LoadData accepts input parameters numRows and numCols for the number of rows and columns in the data file. In general, when working with machine learning, information like this is usually known.

```
static double[][] LoadData(string dataFile, int numRows, int numCols, char delimit)
{
    System.IO.FileStream ifs = new System.IO.FileStream(dataFile, System.IO.FileMode.Open);
    System.IO.StreamReader sr = new System.IO.StreamReader(ifs);
    string line = "";
    string[] tokens = null;
    int i = 0;
    double[][] result = new double[numRows][];
    while ((line = sr.ReadLine()) != null)
    {
        result[i] = new double[numCols];
        tokens = line.Split(delimit);
        for (int j = 0; j < numCols; ++j)
            result[i][j] = double.Parse(tokens[j]);
        ++i;
    }
    sr.Close();
    ifs.Close();
    return result;
}
```

Listing 1-d: Loading Data from a Text File

Calling method LoadData would look something like:

```
string dataFile = "..\\..\\HeightWeight.txt";
double[][] rawData = LoadData(dataFile, 10, 2, ',');
```

An alternative is to programmatically scan the data for the number of rows and columns. In pseudo-code it would look like:

```
numRows := 0
open file
while not EOF
  numRows := numRows + 1
end loop
close file
allocate result array with numRows
open file
while not EOF
  read and parse line with numCols
  allocate curr row of array with numCols
  store line
end loop
```

```
close file
return result matrix
```

Note that even if you are a very experienced programmer, unless you work with scientific or numerical problems often, you may not be familiar with C# array-of-arrays matrices. The matrix coding syntax patterns can take a while to become accustomed to.

The Key Data Structures

The important data structures for the *k*-means clustering program are illustrated in **Figure 1-e**. The array-of-arrays style matrix named data shows how the 10 height-weight data items (sometimes called data tuples) are stored in memory. For example, data[2][0] holds the height of the third person (67 inches) and data[2][1] holds the weight of the third person (99.9 kilograms). In code, data[2] represents the third row of the matrix, which is an array with two cells that holds the height and weight of the third person. There is no convenient way to access an entire column of an array-of-arrays style matrix.

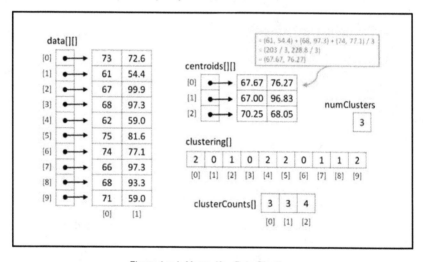

Figure 1-e: k-Means Key Data Structures

Unlike many programming languages, C# supports true, multidimensional arrays. For example, a matrix to hold the same values as the one shown in **Figure 1-e** could be declared and accessed like so:

```
double[,] data = new double[10,2]; // 10 rows, 2 columns
data[0,0] = 73;
data[0,1] = 72.6;
. . .
```

However, using array-of-arrays style matrices is much more common in C# machine learning scenarios, and is generally more convenient because entire rows can be easily accessed.

The demo program maintains an integer array named clustering to hold cluster assignment information. The array indices (0, 1, 2, 3, .. 9) represent indices of the data items. The array cell values { 2, 0, 1, .. 2 } represent the cluster IDs. So, in the figure, data item 0 (which is 73, 72.6) is assigned to cluster 2. Data item 1 (which is 61, 54.4) is assigned to cluster 0. And so on.

There are many alternative ways to store cluster assignment information that trade off efficiency and clarity. For example, you could use an array of List objects, where each List collection holds the indices of data items that belong to the same cluster. As a general rule, the relationship between a machine learning algorithm and the data structures used is very tight, and a change to one of the data structures will require significant changes to the algorithm code.

In **Figure 1-e**, the array clusterCounts holds the number of data items that are assigned to a cluster at any given time during the clustering process. The array indices (0, 1, 2) represent cluster IDs, and the cell values { 3, 3, 4 } represent the number of data items. So, cluster 0 has three data items assigned to it, cluster 1 also has three items, and cluster 2 has four data items.

In **Figure 1-e**, the array-of-arrays matrix centroids holds what you can think of as average data items for each cluster. For example, the centroid of cluster 0 is { 67.67, 76.27 }. The three data items assigned to cluster 0 are items 1, 3, and 6, which are { 61, 54.4 }, { 68, 97.3 } and { 74, 77.1 }. The centroid of a set of vectors is just a vector where each component is the average of the set's values. For example:

centroid[0] = (61 + 68 + 74) / 3 , (54.4 + 97.3 + 77.1) / 3
            = 203 / 3 , 228.8 / 3
            = (67.67, 76.27)

Notice that like the close relationship between an algorithm and the data structures used, there is a very tight coupling among the key data structures. Based on my experience with writing machine learning code, it is essential (for me at least) to have a diagram of all data structures used. Most of the coding bugs I generate are related to the data structures rather than the algorithm logic.

The Clusterer Class

A program-defined class named Clusterer houses the *k*-means clustering algorithm code. The structure of the class is presented in **Listing 1-e**.

```
public class Clusterer
{
    private int numClusters;
    private int[] clustering;
    private double[][] centroids;
    private Random rnd;

    public Clusterer(int numClusters) { . . }
    public int[] Cluster(double[][] data) { . . }
    private bool InitRandom(double[][] data, int maxAttempts) { . . }
    private static int[] Reservoir(int n, int range) { . . }
    private bool UpdateCentroids(double[][] data) { . . }
    private bool UpdateClustering(double[][] data) { . . }
    private static double Distance(double[] tuple, double[] centroid) { . . }
```

```
    private static int MinIndex(double[] distances) { . . }
}
```

Listing 1-e: Program-Defined Clusterer Class

Class Clusterer has four data members, two public methods, and six private helper methods. Three of four data members—variable numClusters, array clustering, and matrix centroids—are explained by the diagram in **Figure 1-e**. The fourth data member, rnd, is a Random object used during the *k*-means initialization process.

Data member rnd is used to generate pseudo-random numbers when data items are initially assigned to random clusters. In most clustering scenarios there is just a single clustering object, but if multiple clustering objects are needed, you may want to consider decorating data member rnd with the static keyword so that there is just a single random number generator shared between clustering object instances.

Class Clusterer exposes just two public methods: a single class constructor, and a method Cluster. Method Cluster calls private helper methods InitRandom, UpdateCentroids, and UpdateClustering. Helper method UpdateClustering calls sub-helper static methods Distance and MinIndex.

The class constructor is short and straightforward:

```
public Clusterer(int numClusters)
{
  this.numClusters = numClusters;
  this.centroids = new double[numClusters][];
  this.rnd = new Random(0);
}
```

The single input parameter, numClusters, is assigned to the class data member of the same name. You may want to perform input error checking to make sure the value of parameter numClusters is greater than or equal to 2. The ability to control when to omit error checking to improve performance is an advantage of writing custom machine learning code.

The constructor allocates the rows of the data member matrix centroids, but cannot allocate the columns because the number of columns will not be known until the data to be clustered is presented. Similarly, array clustering cannot be allocated until the number of data items is known. The Random object is initialized with a seed value of 0, which is arbitrary. Different seed values can produce significantly different clustering results. A common design option is to pass the seed value as an input parameter to the constructor.

If you refer back to **Listing 1-a**, the key calling code is:

```
int numClusters = 3;
Clusterer c = new Clusterer(numClusters);
int[] clustering = c.Cluster(rawData);
```

Notice the Clusterer class does not learn about the data to be clustered until that data is passed to the Cluster method. An important alternative design is to include a reference to the data to be clustered as a class member, and pass the reference to the class constructor. In other words, the Clusterer class would contain an additional field:

```
private double[][] rawData;
```

And the constructor would then be:

```
public Clusterer(int numClusters, double[][] rawData)
{
  this.numClusters = numClusters;
  this.rawData = rawData;
  . . .
}
```

The pros and cons of this design alternative are a bit subtle. One advantage of including the data to be clustered is that it leads to a slightly cleaner design. In my opinion, the two design approaches have roughly equal merit. The decision of whether to pass data to a class constructor or to a public method is a recurring theme when creating custom machine learning code.

The Cluster Method

Method Cluster is presented in **Listing 1-f**. The method accepts a reference to the data to be clustered, which is stored in an array-of-arrays style matrix.

```
public int[] Cluster(double[][] data)
{
  int numTuples = data.Length;
  int numValues = data[0].Length;
  this.clustering = new int[numTuples];

  for (int k = 0; k < numClusters; ++k)
    this.centroids[k] = new double[numValues];

  InitRandom(data);

  Console.WriteLine("\nInitial random clustering:");
  for (int i = 0; i < clustering.Length; ++i)
    Console.Write(clustering[i] + " ");
  Console.WriteLine("\n");

  bool changed = true; // change in clustering?
  int maxCount = numTuples * 10; // sanity check
  int ct = 0;
  while (changed == true && ct < maxCount)
  {
    ++ct;
    UpdateCentroids(data);
    changed = UpdateClustering(data);
  }

  int[] result = new int[numTuples];
```

```
Array.Copy(this.clustering, result, clustering.Length);
    return result;
}
```

Listing 1-f: The Cluster Method

The definition of method Cluster begins with:

```
public int[] Cluster(double[][] data)
{
  int numTuples = data.Length;
  int numValues = data[0].Length;
  this.clustering = new int[numTuples];
. . .
```

The first two statements determine the number of data items to be clustered and the number of values in each data item. Strictly speaking, these two variables are unnecessary, but using them makes the code somewhat easier to understand. Recall that class member array `clustering` and member matrix `centroids` could not be allocated in the constructor because the size of the data to be clustered was not known. So, `clustering` and `centroids` are allocated in method Cluster when the data is first known.

Next, the columns of the data member matrix `centroids` are allocated:

```
for (int k = 0; k < numClusters; ++k)
  this.centroids[k] = new double[numValues];
```

Here, class member `centroids` is referenced using the `this` keyword, but member `numClusters` is referenced without the keyword. In a production environment, you would likely use a standardized coding style.

Next, method Cluster initializes the clustering with random assignments by calling helper method InitRandom:

```
InitRandom(data);
Console.WriteLine("\nInitial random clustering:");
for (int i = 0; i < clustering.Length; ++i)
  Console.Write(clustering[i] + " ");
Console.WriteLine("\n");
```

The k-means initialization process is a major customization point and will be discussed in detail shortly. After the call to InitRandom, the demo program displays the initial clustering to the command shell purely for demonstration purposes. The ability to insert display statements anywhere is another advantage of writing custom machine learning code, compared to using an existing tool or API set where you don't have access to source code.

The heart of method Cluster is the update-centroids, update-clustering loop:

```
bool changed = true;
int maxCount = numTuples * 10; // sanity check
int ct = 0;
while (changed == true && ct <= maxCount)
```

```
{
  ++ct;
  UpdateCentroids(data);
  changed = UpdateClustering(data);
}
```

Helper method UpdateCentroids uses the current clustering to compute the centroid for each cluster. Helper method UpdateClustering then uses the new centroids to reassign each data item to the cluster that is associated with the closest centroid. The method returns false if no data items change clusters.

The k-means algorithm typically reaches a stable clustering very quickly. Mathematically, k-means is guaranteed to converge to a local optimum solution. But this fact does not mean that an implementation of the clustering process is guaranteed to terminate. It is possible, although extremely unlikely, for the algorithm to oscillate, where one data item is repeatedly swapped between two clusters. To prevent an infinite loop, a sanity counter is maintained. Here, the maximum loop count is set to numTuples * 10, which is sufficient in most practical scenarios.

Method Cluster finishes by copying the values in class member array clustering into a local return array. This allows the calling code to access and view the clustering without having to implement a public method along the lines of a routine named GetClustering.

```
. . .
  int[] result = new int[numTuples];
  Array.Copy(this.clustering, result, clustering.Length);
  return result;
}
```

You might want to consider checking the value of variable ct before returning the clustering result. If the value of variable ct equals the value of maxCount, then method Cluster terminated before reaching a stable state, which likely indicates something went very wrong.

Clustering Initialization

The initialization process is critical to the k-means algorithm. After initialization, clustering is essentially deterministic, so a k-means clustering result depends entirely on how the clustering is initialized. There are two main initialization approaches. The demo program assigns each data tuple to a random cluster ID, making sure that each cluster has at least one tuple assigned to it. The definition of method InitRandom begins with:

```
private void InitRandom(double[][] data)
{
  int numTuples = data.Length;
  int clusterID = 0;
  for (int i = 0; i < numTuples; ++i)
  {
    clustering[i] = clusterID++;
    if (clusterID == numClusters)
      clusterID = 0;
  }
. . .
```

The idea is to make sure that each cluster has at least one data tuple assigned. For the demo data with 10 tuples, the code here would initialize class member array clustering to { 0, 1, 2, 0, 1, 2, 0, 1, 2, 0 }. This semi-random initial assignment of data tuples to clusters is fine for most purposes, but it is normal to then further randomize the cluster assignments like so:

```
for (int i = 0; i < numTuples; ++i)
{
  int r = rnd.Next(i, clustering.Length); // pick a cell
  int tmp = clustering[r]; // get the cell value
  clustering[r] = clustering[i]; // swap values
  clustering[i] = tmp;
}
} // InitRandom
```

This randomization code uses an extremely important mini-algorithm called the Fisher-Yates shuffle. The code makes a single scan through the clustering array, swapping pairs of randomly selected values. The algorithm is quite subtle. A common mistake in Fisher-Yates is:

```
int r = rnd.Next(0, clustering.Length); // wrong!
```

Although it is not obvious at all, the bad code generates an apparently random ordering of array values, but in fact the ordering would be strongly biased toward certain patterns.

The second main k-means clustering initialization approach is sometimes called Forgy initialization. The idea is to pick a few actual data tuples to act as initial pseudo-means, and then assign each data tuple to the cluster corresponding to the closest pseudo-mean. In my opinion, research results are not conclusive about which clustering initialization approach is better under which circumstances.

Updating the Centroids

The code for method UpdateClustering begins by computing the current number of data tuples assigned to each cluster:

```
private bool UpdateCentroids(double[][] data)
{
  int[] clusterCounts = new int[numClusters];
  for (int i = 0; i < data.Length; ++i)
  {
    int clusterID = clustering[i];
    ++clusterCounts[clusterID];
  }
. . .
```

The number of tuples assigned to each cluster is needed to compute the average of each centroid component. Here, the clusterCounts array is declared local to method UpdateCentroids. An alternative is to declare clusterCounts as a class member. When writing object-oriented code, it is sometimes difficult to choose between using class members or local variables, and there are very few good, general rules-of-thumb in my opinion.

Next, method UpdateClustering zeroes-out the current cells in the this.centroids matrix:

```
for (int k = 0; k < centroids.Length; ++k)
  for (int j = 0; j < centroids[k].Length; ++j)
    centroids[k][j] = 0.0;
```

An alternative is to use a scratch matrix to perform the calculations. Next, the sums are accumulated:

```
for (int i = 0; i < data.Length; ++i)
{
  int clusterID = clustering[i];
  for (int j = 0; j < data[i].Length; ++j)
    centroids[clusterID][j] += data[i][j]; // accumulate sum
}
```

Even though the code is short, it's a bit tricky and, for me at least, the only way to fully understand what is going on is to sketch a diagram of the data structures, like the one shown in **Figure 1-e**. Method UpdateCentroids concludes by dividing the accumulated sums by the appropriate cluster count:

```
. . .
  for (int k = 0; k < centroids.Length; ++k)
    for (int j = 0; j < centroids[k].Length; ++j)
      centroids[k][j] /= clusterCounts[k]; // danger?
} // UpdateCentroids
```

Notice that if any cluster count has the value 0, a fatal division by zero error will occur. Recall the basic k-means algorithm is:

```
initialize clustering
loop
  update centroids
  update clustering
end loop
```

This implies it is essential that the cluster initialization and cluster update routines ensure that no cluster counts ever become zero. But how can a cluster count become zero? During the k-means processing, data tuples are reassigned to the cluster that corresponds to the closest centroid. Even if each cluster initially has at least one tuple assigned to it, if a data tuple is equally close to two different centroids, the tuple may move to either associated cluster.

Updating the Clustering

The definition of method UpdateClustering starts with:

```
private bool UpdateClustering(double[][] data)
{
  bool changed = false;
  int[] newClustering = new int[clustering.Length];
  Array.Copy(clustering, newClustering, clustering.Length);
  double[] distances = new double[numClusters];
```

. . .

Local variable changed holds the method return value; it's assumed to be false and will be set to true if any tuple changes cluster assignment. Local array newClustering holds the proposed new clustering. The local array named distances holds the distance from a given data tuple to each centroid. For example, if array distances held { 4.0, 1.5, 2.8 }, then the distance from some tuple to cluster 0 is 4.0, the distance from the tuple to centroid 1 is 1.5, and the distance from the tuple to centroid 2 is 2.8. Therefore, the tuple is closest to centroid 1 and would be assigned to cluster 1.

Next, method UpdateClustering does just that with the following code:

```
for (int i = 0; i < data.Length; ++i) // each tuple
{
  for (int k = 0; k < numClusters; ++k)
    distances[k] = Distance(data[i], centroids[k]);

  int newClusterID = MinIndex(distances); // closest centroid
  if (newClusterID != newClustering[i])
  {
    changed = true; // note a new clustering
    newClustering[i] = newClusterID; // accept update
  }
}
```

The key code calls two helper methods: Distance, to compute the distance from a tuple to a centroid, and MinIndex, to identify the cluster ID of the smallest distance. Next, the method checks to see if any data tuples changed cluster assignments:

```
if (changed == false)
  return false;
```

If there is no change to the clustering, then the algorithm has stabilized and UpdateClustering can exit with the current clustering. Another early exit occurs if the proposed new clustering would result in a clustering where one or more clusters have no data tuples assigned to them:

```
int[] clusterCounts = new int[numClusters];
for (int i = 0; i < data.Length; ++i)
{
  int clusterID = newClustering[i];
  ++clusterCounts[clusterID];
}

for (int k = 0; k < numClusters; ++k)
  if (clusterCounts[k] == 0)
    return false; // bad proposed clustering
```

Exiting early when the proposed new clustering would produce an empty cluster is simple and effective, but could lead to a mathematically non-optimal clustering result. An alternative approach is to move a randomly selected data item from a cluster with two or more assigned tuples to the empty cluster. The code to do this is surprisingly tricky. The demo program listing at the end of this chapter shows one possible implementation.

Method UpdateClustering finishes by transferring the values in the proposed new clustering, which is now known to be good, into the class member `clustering` array and returning Boolean true, indicating there was a change in cluster assignments:

```
. . .
  Array.Copy(newClustering, this.clustering, newClustering.Length);
  return true;
} // UpdateClustering
```

Helper method Distance is short but significant:

```
private static double Distance(double[] tuple, double[] centroid)
{
  double sumSquaredDiffs = 0.0;
  for (int j = 0; j < tuple.Length; ++j)
    sumSquaredDiffs += (tuple[j] - centroid[j]) * (tuple[j] - centroid[j]);
  return Math.Sqrt(sumSquaredDiffs);
}
```

Method Distance computes the Euclidean distance between a data tuple and a centroid. For example, suppose some tuple is (70, 80.0) and a centroid is (66, 83.0). The Euclidean distance is:

$$distance = \text{Sqrt}((70 - 66)^2 + (80.0 - 83.0)^2)$$
$$= \text{Sqrt}(16 + 9.0)$$
$$= \text{Sqrt}(25.0)$$
$$= 5.0$$

There are several alternatives to the Euclidean distance that can be used with the k-means algorithm. One of the common alternatives you might want to investigate is called the cosine distance.

Helper method MinIndex locates the index of the smallest value in an array. For the k-means algorithm, this index is equivalent to the cluster ID of the closest centroid:

```
private static int MinIndex(double[] distances)
{
  int indexOfMin = 0;
  double smallDist = distances[0];
  for (int k = 1; k < distances.Length; ++k)
  {
    if (distances[k] < smallDist)
    {
      smallDist = distances[k];
      indexOfMin = k;
    }
  }
  return indexOfMin;
}
```

Even a short and simple routine like method MinIndex has some implementation alternatives to consider. For example, if the method's `static` qualifier is removed, then the reference to `distances.Length` can be replaced with `this.numClusters`.

Summary

The k-means algorithm can be used to group numeric data items. Although it is possible to apply k-means to categorical data by first transforming the data to a numeric form, k-means is not a good choice for categorical data clustering. The main problem is that k-means relies on the notion of distance, which makes sense for numeric data, but usually doesn't make sense for a categorical variable such as color that can take values like red, yellow, and pink.

One important option not presented in the demo program is to normalize the data to be clustered. Normalization transforms the data so that the values in each column have roughly similar magnitudes. Without normalization, columns that have very large magnitude values can dominate columns with small magnitude values. The demo program did not need normalization because the magnitudes of the column values—height in inches and weight in kilograms—were similar.

An algorithm that is closely related to k-means is called k-medoids. Recall that in k-means, a centroid for each cluster is computed, where each centroid is essentially an average data item. Then, each data item is assigned to the cluster associated with the closet centroid. In k-medoids clustering, centroids are calculated, but instead of being an average data item, each centroid is required to be one of the actual data items. Another closely related algorithm is called k-medians clustering. Here, the centroid of each cluster is the median of the data items in the cluster, rather than the average of the data items in the cluster.

Chapter 1 Complete Demo Program Source Code

```
using System;
namespace ClusterNumeric
{
  class ClusterNumProgram
  {
    static void Main(string[] args)
    {
      Console.WriteLine("\nBegin k-means clustering demo\n");

      double[][] rawData = new double[10][];
      rawData[0] = new double[] { 73, 72.6 };
      rawData[1] = new double[] { 61, 54.4 };
      rawData[2] = new double[] { 67, 99.9 };
      rawData[3] = new double[] { 68, 97.3 };
      rawData[4] = new double[] { 62, 59.0 };
      rawData[5] = new double[] { 75, 81.6 };
      rawData[6] = new double[] { 74, 77.1 };
      rawData[7] = new double[] { 66, 97.3 };
      rawData[8] = new double[] { 68, 93.3 };
      rawData[9] = new double[] { 61, 59.0 };

      //double[][] rawData = LoadData("..\\..\\HeightWeight.txt", 10, 2, ',');

      Console.WriteLine("Raw unclustered height (in.) weight (kg.) data:\n");
      Console.WriteLine(" ID    Height    Weight");
      Console.WriteLine("---------------------");
      ShowData(rawData, 1, true, true);

      int numClusters = 3;
      Console.WriteLine("\nSetting numClusters to " + numClusters);

      Console.WriteLine("Starting clustering using k-means algorithm");
      Clusterer c = new Clusterer(numClusters);
      int[] clustering = c.Cluster(rawData);
      Console.WriteLine("Clustering complete\n");

      Console.WriteLine("Final clustering in internal form:\n");
      ShowVector(clustering, true);

      Console.WriteLine("Raw data by cluster:\n");
      ShowClustered(rawData, clustering, numClusters, 1);

      Console.WriteLine("\nEnd k-means clustering demo\n");
      Console.ReadLine();
    }

    static void ShowData(double[][] data, int decimals, bool indices, bool newLine)
    {
      for (int i = 0; i < data.Length; ++i)
      {
        if (indices == true)
          Console.Write(i.ToString().PadLeft(3) + " ");
        for (int j = 0; j < data[i].Length; ++j)
        {
          double v = data[i][j];
          Console.Write(v.ToString("F" + decimals) + "    ");
        }
```

```csharp
      Console.WriteLine("");
    }
    if (newLine == true)
      Console.WriteLine("");
  }

  static void ShowVector(int[] vector, bool newLine)
  {
    for (int i = 0; i < vector.Length; ++i)
      Console.Write(vector[i] + " ");
    if (newLine == true)
      Console.WriteLine("\n");
  }

  static void ShowClustered(double[][] data, int[] clustering,
    int numClusters, int decimals)
  {
    for (int k = 0; k < numClusters; ++k)
    {
      Console.WriteLine("===================");
      for (int i = 0; i < data.Length; ++i)
      {
        int clusterID = clustering[i];
        if (clusterID != k) continue;
        Console.Write(i.ToString().PadLeft(3) + " ");
        for (int j = 0; j < data[i].Length; ++j)
        {
          double v = data[i][j];
          Console.Write(v.ToString("F" + decimals) + " ");
        }
        Console.WriteLine("");
      }
      Console.WriteLine("===================");
    } // k
  }
} // Program

public class Clusterer
{
  private int numClusters; // number of clusters
  private int[] clustering; // index = a tuple, value = cluster ID
  private double[][] centroids; // mean (vector) of each cluster
  private Random rnd; // for initialization

  public Clusterer(int numClusters)
  {
    this.numClusters = numClusters;
    this.centroids = new double[numClusters][];
    this.rnd = new Random(0); // arbitrary seed
  }

  public int[] Cluster(double[][] data)
  {
    int numTuples = data.Length;
    int numValues = data[0].Length;
    this.clustering = new int[numTuples];

    for (int k = 0; k < numClusters; ++k) // allocate each centroid
      this.centroids[k] = new double[numValues];
```

```
InitRandom(data);

Console.WriteLine("\nInitial random clustering:");
for (int i = 0; i < clustering.Length; ++i)
  Console.Write(clustering[i] + " ");
Console.WriteLine("\n");

bool changed = true; // change in clustering?
int maxCount = numTuples * 10; // sanity check
int ct = 0;
while (changed == true && ct <= maxCount)
{
  ++ct; // k-means typically converges very quickly
  UpdateCentroids(data); // no effect if fail
  changed = UpdateClustering(data); // no effect if fail
}

int[] result = new int[numTuples];
Array.Copy(this.clustering, result, clustering.Length);
return result;
} // Cluster

private void InitRandom(double[][] data)
{
  int numTuples = data.Length;

  int clusterID = 0;
  for (int i = 0; i < numTuples; ++i)
  {
    clustering[i] = clusterID++;
    if (clusterID == numClusters)
      clusterID = 0;
  }
  for (int i = 0; i < numTuples; ++i)
  {
    int r = rnd.Next(i, clustering.Length);
    int tmp = clustering[r];
    clustering[r] = clustering[i];
    clustering[i] = tmp;
  }
}

private void UpdateCentroids(double[][] data)
{
  int[] clusterCounts = new int[numClusters];
  for (int i = 0; i < data.Length; ++i)
  {
    int clusterID = clustering[i];
    ++clusterCounts[clusterID];
  }

  // zero-out this.centroids so it can be used as scratch
  for (int k = 0; k < centroids.Length; ++k)
    for (int j = 0; j < centroids[k].Length; ++j)
      centroids[k][j] = 0.0;

  for (int i = 0; i < data.Length; ++i)
  {
    int clusterID = clustering[i];
```

```
      for (int j = 0; j < data[i].Length; ++j)
        centroids[clusterID][j] += data[i][j]; // accumulate sum
  }

  for (int k = 0; k < centroids.Length; ++k)
    for (int j = 0; j < centroids[k].Length; ++j)
      centroids[k][j] /= clusterCounts[k]; // danger?
}

private bool UpdateClustering(double[][] data)
{
  // (re)assign each tuple to a cluster (closest centroid)
  // returns false if no tuple assignments change OR
  // if the reassignment would result in a clustering where
  // one or more clusters have no tuples.

  bool changed = false; // did any tuple change cluster?

  int[] newClustering = new int[clustering.Length]; // proposed result
  Array.Copy(clustering, newClustering, clustering.Length);

  double[] distances = new double[numClusters]; // from tuple to centroids

  for (int i = 0; i < data.Length; ++i) // walk through each tuple
  {
    for (int k = 0; k < numClusters; ++k)
      distances[k] = Distance(data[i], centroids[k]);

    int newClusterID = MinIndex(distances); // find closest centroid
    if (newClusterID != newClustering[i])
    {
      changed = true; // note a new clustering
      newClustering[i] = newClusterID; // accept update
    }
  }

  if (changed == false)
    return false; // no change so bail

  // check proposed clustering cluster counts
  int[] clusterCounts = new int[numClusters];
  for (int i = 0; i < data.Length; ++i)
  {
    int clusterID = newClustering[i];
    ++clusterCounts[clusterID];
  }

  for (int k = 0; k < numClusters; ++k)
    if (clusterCounts[k] == 0)
      return false; // bad clustering

  // alternative: place a random data item into empty cluster
  // for (int k = 0; k < numClusters; ++k)
  // {
  //   if (clusterCounts[k] == 0) // cluster k has no items
  //   {
  //     for (int t = 0; t < data.Length; ++t) // find a tuple to put into cluster k
  //     {
  //       int cid = newClustering[t]; // cluster of t
```

```
//        int ct = clusterCounts[cid]; // how many items are there?
//        if (ct >= 2) // t is in a cluster w/ 2 or more items
//        {
//          newClustering[t] = k; // place t into cluster k
//          ++clusterCounts[k]; // k now has a data item
//          --clusterCounts[cid]; // cluster that used to have t
//          break; // check next cluster
//        }
//      } // t
//    } // cluster count of 0
// } // k

    Array.Copy(newClustering, clustering, newClustering.Length); // update
    return true; // good clustering and at least one change
  } // UpdateClustering

  private static double Distance(double[] tuple, double[] centroid)
  {
    // Euclidean distance between two vectors for UpdateClustering()
    double sumSquaredDiffs = 0.0;
    for (int j = 0; j < tuple.Length; ++j)
      sumSquaredDiffs += (tuple[j] - centroid[j]) * (tuple[j] - centroid[j]);
    return Math.Sqrt(sumSquaredDiffs);
  }

  private static int MinIndex(double[] distances)
  {
    // helper for UpdateClustering() to find closest centroid
    int indexOfMin = 0;
    double smallDist = distances[0];
    for (int k = 1; k < distances.Length; ++k)
    {
      if (distances[k] < smallDist)
      {
        smallDist = distances[k];
        indexOfMin = k;
      }
    }
    return indexOfMin;
  }
} // Clusterer
} // ns
```

Chapter 2 Categorical Data Clustering

Introduction

Data clustering is the process of placing data items into different groups (clusters) in such a way that items in a particular cluster are similar to each other and items in different clusters are different from each other. Once clustered, the data can be examined to find useful information, such as determining what types of items are often purchased together so that targeted advertising can be aimed at customers.

The most common clustering technique is the k-means algorithm. However, k-means is really only applicable when the data items are completely numeric. Clustering data sets that contain categorical attributes such as color, which can take on values like "red" and "blue", is a challenge. One of several approaches for clustering categorical data, or data sets that contain both numeric and categorical data, is to use a concept called category utility (CU).

The CU value for a set of clustered data is a number like 0.3299 that is a measure of how good the particular clustering is. Larger values of CU are better, where the clustering is less likely than a random clustering of the data. There are several clustering algorithms based on CU. This chapter describes a technique called greedy agglomerative category utility clustering (GACUC).

A good way to get a feel for the GACUC clustering algorithm is to examine the screenshot of the demo program shown in **Figure 2-a**. The demo program clusters a data set of seven items into two groups. Each data item represents a gemstone. Each item has three attributes: color (red, blue, green, or yellow), size (small, medium, or large), and heaviness (false or true).

The final clustering of the seven data items is:

```
Index  Color    Size     Heavy
-----------------------------------
  0    Blue     Small    False
  2    Red      Large    False
  3    Red      Small    True
  6    Red      Large    False
-----------------------------------
  1    Green    Medium   True
  4    Green    Medium   False
  5    Yellow   Medium   False
-----------------------------------
CU = 0.3299
```

Even though it's surprisingly difficult to describe exactly what a good clustering is, most people would likely agree that the final clustering shown is the best way to place the seven data items into two clusters.

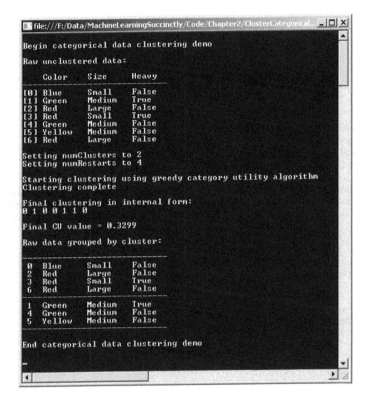

Figure 2-a: Clustering Categorical Data

Clustering using the GACUC algorithm, like most clustering algorithms, requires the user to specify the number of clusters in advance. However, unlike most clustering algorithms, GACUC provides a metric of clustering goodness, so you can try clustering with different numbers of clusters and easily compare the results.

Understanding Category Utility

The key to implementing and customizing the GACUC clustering algorithm is understanding category utility. Data clustering involves solving two main problems. The first problem is defining exactly what makes a good clustering of data. The second problem is determining an effective technique to search through all possible combinations of clustering to find the best clustering.

CU addresses the first problem. CU is a very clever metric that defines a clustering goodness. Small values of CU indicate poor clustering and larger values indicate better clustering. As far as I've been able to determine, CU was first defined by M. Gluck and J. Corter in a 1985 research paper titled "Information, Uncertainty, and the Utility of Categories."

The mathematical equation for CU is a bit intimidating at first glance:

$$CU(C) = \frac{1}{m} \sum_{k=0}^{m-1} P(C_k) \left[\sum_i \sum_j P(A_i = V_{ij} \mid C_k)^2 - \sum_i \sum_j P(A_i = V_{ij})^2 \right]$$

The equation is simpler than it first appears. Uppercase C is an overall clustering. Lowercase m is the number of clusters. Lowercase k is a zero-based cluster index. Uppercase P means "probability of." Uppercase A means attribute (such as color). Uppercase V means attribute value (such as red).

The term inside the double summation on the right represents the probability of guessing an attribute value purely by chance. The term inside the double summation on the left represents the probability of guessing an attribute value for the given clustering. So, the larger the difference, the less likely the clustering occurred by chance.

Computing category utility is probably best understood by example. Suppose the data set to be clustered is the one shown at the top of **Figure 2-a**, and you want to compute the CU of this (non-best) clustering:

```
k = 0
- - - - - - - - - - - - - - - - - - - - -
Red       Large    False
Green     Medium   False
Yellow    Medium   False
Red       Large    False

k = 1
- - - - - - - - - - - - - - - - - - - - -
Blue      Small    False
Green     Medium   True
Red       Small    True
```

The first step is to compute the $P(C_k)$, which are the probabilities of each cluster. For $k = 0$, because there are seven tuples in the data set and four of them are in cluster 0, $P(C_0) = 4/7 = 0.5714$. Similarly, $P(C_1) = 3/7 = 0.4286$.

The second step is to compute the double summation on the right in the CU equation, called the unconditional term. The computation is the sum of N terms where N is the total number of different attribute values in the data set, and goes like this:

```
Red:     (3/7)² = 0.1837
Blue:    (1/7)² = 0.0204
Green:   (2/7)² = 0.0816
Yellow:  (1/7)² = 0.0204
Small:   (2/7)² = 0.0816
Medium:  (3/7)² = 0.1837
Large:   (2/7)² = 0.0816
```

```
False:  (5/7)² = 0.5102
True :  (2/7)² = 0.0816
Unconditional sum = 0.1837 + 0.0204 + . . . + 0.0816 = 1.2449 (rounded)
```

The third step is to compute the double summation on the left, called the conditional probability terms. There are m sums (where m is the number of clusters), each of which has N terms.

For $k = 0$ the computation goes:

```
Red:    (2/4)² = 0.2500
Blue :  (0/4)² = 0.0000
Green:  (1/4)² = 0.0625
Yellow: (1/4)² = 0.0625
Small:  (0/4)² = 0.0000
Medium: (2/4)² = 0.2500
Large:  (2/4)² = 0.2500
False:  (4/4)² = 1.0000
True :  (0/4)² = 0.0000
```

Conditional $k = 0$ sum = 0.2500 + 0.0000 + . . . + 0.2500 = 1.8750

For $k = 1$ the computation is:

```
Red:    (1/3)² = 0.1111
Blue :  (1/3)² = 0.1111
Green:  (1/3)² = 0.1111
Yellow: (0/3)² = 0.0000
Small:  (2/3)² = 0.4444
Medium: (1/3)² = 0.1111
Large:  (0/3)² = 0.0000
False:  (1/3)² = 0.1111
True :  (2/3)² = 0.4444
```

Conditional $k = 1$ sum = 0.1111 + 0.1111 + . . . + 0.4444 = 1.4444 (rounded)

The last step is to combine the computed sums according to the CU equation:

CU = 1/2 * [0.5714 * (1.8750 - 1.2449) + 0.4286 * (1.4444 - 1.2449)]

= 0.2228 (rounded)

Notice the CU of this non-optimal clustering, 0.2228, is less than the CU of the optimal clustering, 0.3299, shown in **Figure 2-a**. The key point is that for any clustering of a data set containing categorical data, it is possible to compute a value that describes how good the clustering is.

Understanding the GACUC Algorithm

After defining a way to measure clustering goodness, the second challenging step when clustering categorical data is coming up with a technique to search through all possible clusterings. In general, it is not feasible to examine every possible clustering of a data set. For example, even for a data set with only 100 tuples, and $m = 2$ clusters, there are $2^{100} / 2! = 2^{99} =$ 633,825,300,114,114,700,748,351,602,688 possible clusterings. Even if you could somehow examine one trillion clusterings per second, it would take roughly 19 billion years to check them all. For comparison, the age of the universe is estimated to be about 14 billion years.

The GACUC algorithm uses what is called a greedy agglomerative approach. The idea is to begin by seeding each cluster with a single data tuple. Then for each remaining tuple, determine which cluster, if the current tuple were added to it, would yield the best overall clustering. Then the tuple that gives the best CU is actually assigned to that cluster.

Expressed in pseudo-code:

```
assign just one data tuple to each cluster
loop each remaining tuple
  for each cluster
    compute CU if tuple were to be assigned to cluster
    save proposed CU
  end for
  determine which cluster assignment would have given best CU
  actually assign tuple to that cluster
end loop
```

The algorithm is termed *greedy* because the best choice (tuple-cluster assignment in this case) at any given state is always selected. The algorithm is termed agglomerative because the final solution (overall clustering in this case) is built up one item at a time.

This algorithm does not guarantee that the optimal clustering will be found. The final clustering produced by the GACUC algorithm depends on which m tuples are selected as initial seed tuples, and the order in which the remaining tuples are examined. But because the result of any clustering has a goodness metric, CU, you can use what is called "restart". In pseudo-code:

```
loop n times
  cluster all data tuples, computing the current CU
  if current CU > best CU
    save current clustering
    best CU := current CU
  end if
end loop
return best clustering found
```

It turns out that selecting an initial data tuple for each cluster is not trivial. One naive approach would be to simply select m random tuples as the seeds. However, if the seed tuples are similar to each other, then the resulting clustering could be poor. A better approach for selecting initial tuples for each cluster is to select m tuples that are as different as possible from each other.

There are several ways to define how a set of data tuples differ. The simplest approach is to count the total number of attribute values that differ when each possible pair of tuples is examined. This is called the Hamming distance. For example, consider these three tuples:

```
[0]  Red      Large    False
[1]  Green    Medium   False
[2]  Yellow   Medium   False
```

Looking at the color attribute, items 0 and 1 differ, 0 and 2 differ, and 1 and 2 differ. Looking at the size attribute, items 0 and 1 differ, and items 0 and 2 differ. Looking at the heaviness attribute, no pairs of tuples differ. So there are a total of 3 + 2 + 0 = 5 differences. Larger values for the difference metric mean more dissimilarity, which is better for choosing the initial tuples to be assigned to clusters.

Now another, but relatively minor, problem arises. In most situations it isn't feasible to examine all possible sets of initial tuples. If there are T data tuples and m clusters, then there are Choose(T, m) ways to select m tuples from the set of T tuples. For example, if T = 500 and m = 10, then there are Choose(500, 10) = 500! / 10! * 490! = 245,810,588,801,891,098,700 possible sets of initial tuples to examine. GACUC uses this approach to select a few random sets of initial tuples to examine, rather than try to examine all possible sets.

Demo Program Overall Structure

To create the demo, I launched Visual Studio and created a new C# console application and named it ClusterCategorical. After the template code loaded in the editor, I removed all using statements at the top of the source code, except for the references to the top-level System and the Collections.Generic namespaces.

In the Solution Explorer window, I renamed file Program.cs to the more descriptive ClusterCatProgram.cs, and Visual Studio automatically renamed class Program to ClusterCatProgram.

The overall structure of the demo program, with a few minor edits to save space, is presented in **Listing 2-a**. Note that in order to keep the size of the example code small, and the main ideas as clear as possible, all normal error checking is omitted.

```csharp
using System;
using System.Collections.Generic;
namespace ClusterCategorical
{
  class ClusterCatProgram
  {
    static void Main(string[] args)
    {
      Console.WriteLine("Begin categorical data clustering demo");

      string[][] rawData = new string[7][];
      rawData[0] = new string[] { "Blue", "Small", "False" };
      rawData[1] = new string[] { "Green", "Medium", "True" };
      rawData[2] = new string[] { "Red", "Large", "False" };
      rawData[3] = new string[] { "Red", "Small", "True" };
      rawData[4] = new string[] { "Green", "Medium", "False" };
```

```
        rawData[5] = new string[] { "Yellow", "Medium", "False" };
        rawData[6] = new string[] { "Red", "Large", "False" };

        Console.WriteLine("Raw unclustered data: ");
        Console.WriteLine("    Color    Size    Heavy");
        Console.WriteLine("----------------------------");
        ShowData(rawData);

        int numClusters = 2;
        Console.WriteLine("Setting numClusters to " + numClusters);
        int numRestarts = 4;
        Console.WriteLine("Setting numRestarts to " + numRestarts);

        Console.WriteLine("Starting clustering using greedy CU algorithm");
        CatClusterer cc = new CatClusterer(numClusters, rawData);
        double cu;
        int[] clustering = cc.Cluster(numRestarts, out cu);
        Console.WriteLine("Clustering complete");

        Console.WriteLine("Final clustering in internal form: ");
        ShowVector(clustering, true);

        Console.WriteLine("Final CU value = " + cu.ToString("F4"));

        Console.WriteLine("Raw data grouped by cluster: ");
        ShowClustering(numClusters, clustering, rawData);

        Console.WriteLine("End categorical data clustering demo\n");
        Console.ReadLine();
      } // Main

      static void ShowData(string[][] matrix) { . . }
      static void ShowVector(int[] vector, bool newLine) { . . }
      static void ShowClustering(int numClusters, int[] clustering,
        string[][] rawData) { . . }
    } // Program

    public class CatClusterer { . . }

} // ns
```

Listing 2-a: Categorical Data Clustering Demo Program Structure

All the clustering logic is contained in a single program-defined class named CatClusterer. All the program logic is contained in the Main method. The Main method begins by setting up seven hard-coded, color-size-heaviness data items in an array-of-arrays style matrix:

```
static void Main(string[] args)
{
  Console.WriteLine("\nBegin categorical data clustering demo\n");
  string[][] rawData = new string[7][];
  rawData[0] = new string[] { "Blue", "Small", "False" };
  rawData[1] = new string[] { "Green", "Medium", "True" };
  rawData[2] = new string[] { "Red", "Large", "False" };
  rawData[3] = new string[] { "Red", "Small", "True" };
  rawData[4] = new string[] { "Green", "Medium", "False" };
  rawData[5] = new string[] { "Yellow", "Medium", "False" };
```

```
rawData[6] = new string[] { "Red", "Large", "False" };
. . .
```

In a non-demo scenario, you would likely have data stored in a text file and would load the data into memory using a helper function. After displaying the raw string data matrix using helper method ShowData, the demo program prepares the clustering parameters:

```
int numClusters = 2;
Console.WriteLine("\nSetting numClusters to " + numClusters);
int numRestarts = 4;
Console.WriteLine("Setting numRestarts to " + numRestarts);
```

Variable numRestarts holds the number of times the GACUC algorithm will be called, looking for the clustering that gives the largest CU value. Larger values of numRestarts increase the chances of finding the optimal clustering, but at the expense of time. A rule of thumb that often works well in practice is to set numRestarts to the square root of the number of data items.

The calling interface is simple:

```
CatClusterer cc = new CatClusterer(numClusters, rawData);
double cu;
int[] clustering = cc.Cluster(numRestarts, out cu);
ShowVector(clustering, true);
Console.WriteLine("Final CU value = " + cu.ToString("F4"));
```

A CatClusterer object is instantiated and its Cluster method is called. Behind the scenes, method Cluster calls a method ClusterOnce several (numRestarts) times, keeping track of the best clustering found. That best clustering, and its associated CU value, are returned.

In the demo program, the final best clustering is stored into an array called clustering and is encoded as { 0, 1, 0, 0, 1, 1, 0 }. This means data tuple 0 is assigned to cluster 0, data tuple 1 is assigned to cluster 1, data tuple 2 is assigned to cluster 0, and so on. The final CU value of the best clustering found is stored into out-parameter cu and is 0.3299.

The demo program concludes by calling helper method ShowClustering to display the raw data, arranged by cluster:

```
. . .
  Console.WriteLine("\nRaw data grouped by cluster:\n");
  ShowClustering(numClusters, clustering, rawData);
  Console.WriteLine("\nEnd categorical data clustering demo\n");
  Console.ReadLine();
} // Main
```

The Key Data Structures

The important data structures for the GACUC categorical data clustering program are illustrated in **Figure 2-b**. The array-of-arrays style matrix named rawData shows the data tuples where attribute values (like red) are in string form. Matrix tuplesAsInt holds the same data but where each attribute value has been converted to a zero-based index (like 2). In situations with very large data sets or limited machine memory, an alternative design is to store string-to-integer encoding, for example, by using a generic Dictionary collection for each attribute column.

The GACUC algorithm computes category utility many times. It would be possible to compute CU from scratch each time, which would involve scanning the entire data set and counting the number of attribute values assigned to each cluster. But a far more efficient approach is to store the current count of each attribute value in a data structure, and then update the data structure as each data tuple is assigned to a cluster. Data structure valueCounts stores this information.

The first index of valueCounts is an attribute, like color. The second index is an attribute value, like red. The third index is a cluster ID, like 0. The cell value is the count. For example, if cell valueCounts[0][2][0] has value 3, this means there are three data tuples assigned to cluster 0, where color (0) has value red (2).

The cell in valueCounts where the third index has value numClusters holds the sum of assigned tuples for all clusters for the associated attribute value. For example, valueCounts[0][2][2] holds the number of tuples assigned where color = red.

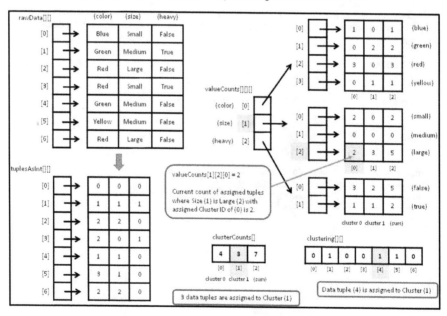

Figure 2-b: GACUC Clustering Algorithm Key Data Structures

The array clusterCounts holds the number of data tuples assigned to each cluster at any point during the algorithm, and also the total number of tuples that have been assigned. For example, if clusterCounts has values { 2, 3, 5 }, then two tuples have been assigned to cluster 0, three tuples have been assigned to cluster 1, and a total of five tuples have been assigned.

The CatClusterer Class

A program-defined class named CatClusterer houses the GACUC algorithm code. The structure of the class is presented in **Listing 2-b**.

```
public class CatClusterer
{
  private int numClusters;
  private int[] clustering;
  private int[][] dataAsInts;
  private int[][][] valueCounts;
  private int[] clusterCounts;
  private Random rnd;

  public CatClusterer(int numClusters, string[][] rawData) { . . }
  public int[] Cluster(int numRestarts, out double catUtility) { . . }

  private int[] ClusterOnce(int seed, out double catUtility)

  private void MakeDataMatrix(string[][] rawData)
  private void Allocate() { . . }
  private void Initialize() { . . }
  private double CategoryUtility() { . . }
  private static int MaxIndex(double[] cus) { . . }
  private void Shuffle(int[] indices) { . . }
  private void Assign(int dataIndex, int clusterID) { . . }
  private void Unassign(int dataIndex, int clusterID) { . . }
  private int[] GetGoodIndices(int numTrials) { . . }
  private int[] Reservoir(int n, int range) { . . }
}
```

Listing 2-b: Program-Defined CatClusterer Class

Class CatClusterer has six private data members, which are illustrated in **Figure 2-b**. For most developers, including me, having a diagram of the key data structures is essential when writing machine learning code. Class member rnd is used when generating candidate sets of initial tuples to be assigned to clusters, and when iterating through the remaining tuples in a random order.

The class exposes just two public methods: a constructor, and the clustering method. Helper method ClusterOnce performs one pass of the GACUC algorithm, returning the clustering found and the associated CU as an out-parameter. Method Cluster calls ClusterOnce numRestart times and returns the best clustering and CU found.

Helper methods MakeDataMatrix and Allocate are called by the class constructor. Method MakeDataMatrix accepts the matrix of raw string data to be clustered and returns the equivalent zero-based integer encoded matrix. An important design alternative is to preprocess the raw data and save the integer representation as a text file. Method Allocate allocates memory for the key data structures and is just a convenience to keep the constructor code tidy.

Method ClusterOnce, which does most of the work, calls helper methods GetGoodIndices, Assign, Unassign, Shuffle, and MaxIndex. Method GetGoodIndices generates initial data tuples that are different from each other. Assign updates all data structures to assign a tuple to a cluster. Unassign reverses the action of Assign. Method Shuffle is used to present data tuples in random order. Method MaxIndex is used to find the best proposed cluster assignment.

Private method Reservoir is a sub-helper called by helper method GetGoodIndices. Method Reservoir uses a mini-algorithm called reservoir sampling to find n distinct array indices. The CatClusterer class constructor is short:

```
public CatClusterer(int numClusters, string[][] rawData)
{
  this.numClusters = numClusters;
  MakeDataMatrix(rawData);
  Allocate();
}
```

A recurring theme when designing machine learning code is the decision of whether to pass the source data to the constructor or to the primary public method. Here, the data is passed to the constructor so that helper MakeDataMatrix can create the internal integer-form dataAsInts matrix.

The Cluster Method

Method Cluster is presented in **Listing 2-c**. Notice that the method does not accept a parameter representing the data to be clustered; the data is assumed to be available as a class member.

```
public int[] Cluster(int numRestarts, out double catUtility)
{
  int numRows = dataAsInts.Length;
  double currCU, bestCU = 0.0;
  int[] bestClustering = new int[numRows];
  for (int start = 0; start < numRestarts; ++start)
  {
    int seed = start; // use the start index as rnd seed
    int[] currClustering = ClusterOnce(seed, out currCU);
    if (currCU > bestCU)
    {
      bestCU = currCU;
      Array.Copy(currClustering, bestClustering, numRows);
    }
  }
  catUtility = bestCU;
  return bestClustering;
}
```

Listing 2-c: The Cluster Method

Method Cluster is essentially a wrapper around method ClusterOnce. Notice that the randomization seed value passed to method ClusterOnce is the value of current iteration variable, start. This trick is a common design pattern when using a restart algorithm so that the worker method does not return the same result in each iteration.

The definition of method ClusterOnce begins with:

```
private int[] ClusterOnce(int seed, out double catUtility)
{
  this.rnd = new Random(seed);
  Initialize();
. . .
```

Helper method Initialize performs three tasks. First, the values in the clustering array are all set to -1. This allows the algorithm to know whether a data tuple has been assigned to a cluster or not. Second, the values in clusterCounts are set to 0 to reset the array, which holds counts from any previous call to ClusterOnce. Third, the values in data structure valueCounts are set to 0.

Next, method ClusterOnce selects the first tuples and assigns them to clusters:

```
int numTrials = dataAsInts.Length;
int[] goodIndexes = GetGoodIndices(numTrials);
for (int k = 0; k < numClusters; ++k)
  Assign(goodIndexes[k], k);
```

Method GetGoodIndices returns numClusters data indices where the data tuples are different from each other. As explained earlier, it's usually not possible to examine all possible candidate sets of initial tuples, so numTrials of sets are examined. After these good indices (the data tuples are different) are found, their associated data tuples are assigned to clusters.

A short example will help clarify. For the demo data, with seven data tuples and number of clusters set to three, method GetGoodIndices might return { 6, 0, 1 }. These are the indices of three data items that are very different from each other, as defined by Hamming distance:

```
[6]  Red     Large   False
[0]  Blue    Small   False
[1]  Green   Medium  True
```

These three tuples, 6, 0, and 1, are assigned to clusters 0, 1, and 2, respectively. The resulting clustering data member would then be:

```
1    2    -1   -1   -1   -1   0    (cluster ID)
[0]  [1]  [2]  [3]  [4]  [5]  [6]  (tuple index)
```

Next, the order of the data tuples is scrambled so that they will be presented in a random order:

```
int numRows = dataAsInts.Length;
int[] rndSequence = new int[numRows];
for (int i = 0; i < numRows; ++i)
  rndSequence[i] = i;
Shuffle(rndSequence);
```

Helper method Shuffle uses the Fisher-Yates algorithm to shuffle the data tuple indices. Use of the Fisher-Yates shuffle is very common in machine learning code.

At this point, the clustering algorithm walks through each tuple. If the current tuple has not been assigned to a cluster (the value in clustering will be -1 if unassigned), each possible value of cluster ID is examined, and the one cluster ID that gave the best clustering (the largest value of CU) is associated with the current tuple:

```
for (int t = 0; t < numRows; ++t)  // walk through each tuple
{
  int idx = rndSequence[t]; // index of data tuple to process
  if (clustering[idx] != -1) continue;  // already clustered

  double[] candidateCU = new double[numClusters];

  for (int k = 0; k < numClusters; ++k) // each possible cluster
  {
    Assign(idx, k); // tentative cluster assignment
    candidateCU[k] = CategoryUtility(); // compute and save the CU
    Unassign(idx, k); // undo tentative assignment
  }

  int bestK = MaxIndex(candidateCU);  // greedy. index is a cluster ID
  Assign(idx, bestK); // now we know which cluster gave the best CU
} // each tuple
```

At this point, all data tuples have been assigned to a cluster. Method ClusterOnce computes the final category utility and returns the clustering as an explicit return value, and the CU as an out-parameter:

```
. . .
  catUtility = CategoryUtility();
  int[] result = new int[numRows];
  Array.Copy(this.clustering, result, numRows);
  return result;
}
```

The CategoryUtility Method

The heart of the GACUC categorical data clustering algorithm is the method that computes category utility for a given clustering of data. Method CategoryUtility is relatively simple because it uses the precomputed counts stored in data structures valueCounts and clusterCounts.

The definition begins by computing the $P(C_k)$ terms, the probabilities of each cluster:

```
private double CategoryUtility() // called by ClusterOnce
{
  int numTuplesAssigned = clusterCounts[clusterCounts.Length - 1];
  double[] clusterProbs = new double[this.numClusters];
  for (int k = 0; k < numClusters; ++k)
    clusterProbs[k] = (clusterCounts[k] * 1.0) / numTuplesAssigned;
  . . .
```

Next, the single unconditional term (the sum of the unconditional probabilities) is computed:

```
double unconditional = 0.0;
for (int i = 0; i < valueCounts.Length; ++i)
{
  for (int j = 0; j < valueCounts[i].Length; ++j)
  {
    int sum = valueCounts[i][j][numClusters]; // last cell holds sum
    double p = (sum * 1.0) / numTuplesAssigned;
    unconditional += (p * p);
  }
}
```

Next, the numCluster conditional terms (the sums of conditional probabilities) are computed:

```
double[] conditionals = new double[numClusters];
for (int k = 0; k < numClusters; ++k)
{
  for (int i = 0; i < valueCounts.Length; ++i) // each att
  {
    for (int j = 0; j < valueCounts[i].Length; ++j) // each value
    {
      double p = (valueCounts[i][j][k] * 1.0) / clusterCounts[k];
      conditionals[k] += (p * p);
    }
  }
}
```

With the pieces of the puzzle computed, method CategoryUtility combines them according to the mathematical definition of category utility:

```
. . .
  double summation = 0.0;
  for (int k = 0; k < numClusters; ++k)
    summation += clusterProbs[k] * (conditionals[k] - unconditional);
  return summation / numClusters;
}
```

Method CategoryUtility is an internal method in the sense that it assumes all needed counts are available. You might want to consider writing a standalone public-scope version that creates and initializes local versions of valueCounts and clusterCounts, scans the clustering array and uses the dataAsInts matrix to populate the counts data structures, and then uses the counts to compute CU.

Clustering Initialization

The clustering initialization process is the primary customization point for the GACUC categorical data clustering algorithm. After initialization, GACUC clustering is deterministic, so the clustering result depends entirely on initialization. Initialization is implemented in method GetGoodIndices.

The method's definition begins:

```
private int[] GetGoodIndices(int numTrials)
{
  int numRows = dataAsInts.Length;
  int numCols = dataAsInts[0].Length;
  int[] result = new int[numClusters];
. . .
```

The goal is to find the indices of data tuples that are different from each other. Because it is not possible in most scenarios to examine all possible sets of candidate data tuples, parameter numTrials holds the number of times to examine randomly selected sets.

Even though not all possible sets of initial tuples can be examined, in general it is possible to compare all possible pairs of tuples within a set of candidates:

```
int largestDiff = -1;
for (int trial = 0; trial < numTrials; ++trial)
{
  int[] candidates = Reservoir(numClusters, numRows);
  int numDifferences = 0; // for these candidates

  for (int i = 0; i < candidates.Length - 1; ++i) // all possible pairs
  {
    for (int j = i + 1; j < candidates.Length; ++j)
    {
      int aRow = candidates[i];
      int bRow = candidates[j];

      for (int col = 0; col < numCols; ++col)
        if (dataAsInts[aRow][col] != dataAsInts[bRow][col])
          ++numDifferences;
    } // j
  } // i
. . .
```

This idea may be a bit confusing. Suppose the source data to cluster has 500 data items and the number of clusters is set to 3. There are Choose(500, 3) = 20,708,500 possible candidate sets of the initial three tuples, which is a lot. Suppose each data tuple has four attributes. To compare all possible pairs of any set of three tuples, there are Choose(3, 2) * 4 = 12 comparisons required, which is quite feasible.

In situations where the number of clusters is very large and the number of attributes is also large, you can modify GetGoodIndices to examine only adjacent pairs of the candidate tuples. The program listing at the end of this chapter provides example code for this.

The second initialization option is to use an alternative to the Hamming distance to measure the difference between two data tuples. Options you may wish to explore include metrics called cosine similarity, Goodall similarity, and Smirnov similarity.

Method GetGoodIndices concludes by tracking whether the current number of value differences is greater than the best (largest) found so far, and if so, saving the candidate set of tuple indices:

```
. . .
    if (numDifferences > largestDiff)
    {
      largestDiff = numDifferences;
      Array.Copy(candidates, result, numClusters);
    }
  } // trial
  return result;
}
```

Reservoir Sampling

Method GetGoodIndices calls a helper method named Reservoir. This utility method returns n random, distinct values from 0 to r - 1, which corresponds to n distinct array indices. Returning n random, distinct array indices is a very common machine learning task, and one that is surprisingly interesting.

For the demo program, with seven data tuples with indices 0 through 6 (so r = 7), and the number of clusters set to three (so n = 3), method GetGoodIndices must generate three distinct values from 0 through 6. There are three common ways to generate n random distinct array indices: brute force, shuffle-select, and reservoir sampling.

In pseudo-code, the brute force technique to generate n random integers between 0 and r - 1 is:

```
loop t times
  select n random integers between [0, r-1]
  if all n integers are different
    return the n integers
  end if
  // try again
end loop
return failure
```

The problem with the brute force approach is that there is no guarantee that you'll ever get n different values. However, brute force is very effective when the number of integers to generate (n) is very, very small compared to the range (r). For example, if the goal is to select n = 3 integers between 0 and 9999, the chances of getting a duplicate value among three random values is small.

In pseudo-code, the shuffle-select technique is:

```
create a scratch array of sequential integers from 0 through r-1
shuffle the values in the array (using Fisher-Yates)
select and return the first n values in the shuffled array
```

The problem with the shuffle-select approach is that it uses extra memory for the scratch array. However, shuffle-select is simple and effective when n is small (say, less than 1,000).

The demo program uses a very clever algorithm called reservoir sampling. In pseudo-code:

```
create a small result array of sequential integers from 0 through n-1
loop for t := n to r-1
  generate a random integer j between [0, t]
  if j < n
  set result[j] := t
end loop
return result
```

Reservoir sampling is not at all obvious, and is a rare example where the actual code is probably easier to understand than pseudo-code. The code for method Reservoir is:

```
private int[] Reservoir(int n, int range)
{
  // select n random indices between [0, range)
  int[] result = new int[n];
  for (int i = 0; i < n; ++i)
    result[i] = i;

  for (int t = n; t < range; ++t)
  {
    int j = rnd.Next(0, t + 1);
    if (j < n)
      result[j] = t;
  }
  return result;
}
```

Suppose the goal is to generate $n = 3$ random distinct integers between 0 and 6, inclusive. The result array is initialized to { 0, 1, 2 }. The first time through the algorithm's loop, $t = 3$. A random j is generated between 0 and 3 inclusive. Let's suppose it is $j = 2$. Because $(j = 2) < (n = 3)$, result[$j = 2$] is set to $t = 3$, so the result array is now { 0, 1, 3 }.

The second time through the loop, $t = 4$. Suppose generated $j = 0$. Because $(j = 0) < (n = 3)$, result[$j = 0$] is set to $t = 4$ and result is now { 4, 1, 3 }.

The third time through the loop, $t = 5$. Suppose generated $j = 4$. Because $(j = 4)$ is not less than $(n = 3)$, result is not changed and remains { 4, 1, 3 }.

The fourth time through the loop, $t = 6$. Suppose generated $j = 1$. Because $(j = 1) < (n = 3)$, result[$j = 1$] is set to 6 and result is now { 4, 6, 3 }. The t-loop terminates and result is returned.

Clustering Mixed Data

The GACUC clustering algorithm is intended for categorical data items, but it can also be used to cluster data that contains a mixture of numeric and categorical data. The idea is to first convert numeric data into categorical data. For example, suppose the data items to be clustered represent people, and each item has attributes (sex, age, job). For example, the first two data items might be:

```
male, 28.0, engineer
female, 52.0, accountant
```

If you convert the raw age data so that ages 0 through 21 are low, ages 22 through 45 are medium, and ages 46 through 99 are high, the data items become:

```
male, medium, engineer
female, high, accountant
```

Now the data is all categorical and the GACUC algorithm can be used. Converting numeric data to categorical data is called *discretizing* the data, or binning the data.

With this example data, the GACUC algorithm does not take into account the fact that category high is closer to category medium than to category low. An unexplored option is to modify the GACUC algorithm to use categorical data closeness information.

Chapter 2 Complete Demo Program Source Code

```
using System;
using System.Collections.Generic;
namespace ClusterCategorical
{
  class ClusterCatProgram
  {
    static void Main(string[] args)
    {
      Console.WriteLine("\nBegin categorical data clustering demo\n");

      string[][] rawData = new string[7][];

      rawData[0] = new string[] { "Blue", "Small", "False" };
      rawData[1] = new string[] { "Green", "Medium", "True" };
      rawData[2] = new string[] { "Red", "Large", "False" };
      rawData[3] = new string[] { "Red", "Small", "True" };
      rawData[4] = new string[] { "Green", "Medium", "False" };
      rawData[5] = new string[] { "Yellow", "Medium", "False" };
      rawData[6] = new string[] { "Red", "Large", "False" };

      Console.WriteLine("Raw unclustered data:\n");
      Console.WriteLine("    Color    Size    Heavy");
      Console.WriteLine("---------------------------");
      ShowData(rawData);

      int numClusters = 2;
      Console.WriteLine("\nSetting numClusters to " + numClusters);
      int numRestarts = 4;
      Console.WriteLine("Setting numRestarts to " + numRestarts);

      Console.WriteLine("\nStarting clustering using greedy category utility");
      CatClusterer cc = new CatClusterer(numClusters, rawData); // restart version
      double cu;
      int[] clustering = cc.Cluster(numRestarts, out cu);
      Console.WriteLine("Clustering complete\n");

      Console.WriteLine("Final clustering in internal form:");
      ShowVector(clustering, true);

      Console.WriteLine("Final CU value = " + cu.ToString("F4"));

      Console.WriteLine("\nRaw data grouped by cluster:\n");
      ShowClustering(numClusters, clustering, rawData);

      Console.WriteLine("\nEnd categorical data clustering demo\n");
      Console.ReadLine();
    } // Main

    static void ShowData(string[][] matrix) // for tuples
    {
      for (int i = 0; i < matrix.Length; ++i)
      {
        Console.Write("[" + i + "] ");
        for (int j = 0; j < matrix[i].Length; ++j)
          Console.Write(matrix[i][j].ToString().PadRight(8) + " ");
        Console.WriteLine("");
      }
```

```
    }

    public static void ShowVector(int[] vector, bool newLine) // for clustering
    {
      for (int i = 0; i < vector.Length; ++i)
        Console.Write(vector[i] + " ");
      Console.WriteLine("");
      if (newLine == true)
        Console.WriteLine("");
    }

    static void ShowClustering(int numClusters, int[] clustering, string[][] rawData)
    {
      Console.WriteLine("----------------------------");
      for (int k = 0; k < numClusters; ++k) // display by cluster
      {
        for (int i = 0; i < rawData.Length; ++i) // each tuple
        {
          if (clustering[i] == k) // curr tuple i belongs to curr cluster k
          {
            Console.Write(i.ToString().PadLeft(2) + "  ");
            for (int j = 0; j < rawData[i].Length; ++j)
            {
              Console.Write(rawData[i][j].ToString().PadRight(8) + " ");
            }
            Console.WriteLine("");
          }
        }
        Console.WriteLine("----------------------------");
      }
    }

  } // Program

  public class CatClusterer
  {
    private int numClusters; // number of clusters
    private int[] clustering; // index = a tuple, value = cluster ID
    private int[][] dataAsInts; // ex: red = 0, blue = 1, green = 2
    private int[][][] valueCounts; // scratch to compute CU [att][val][count](sum)
    private int[] clusterCounts; // number tuples assigned to each cluster (sum)
    private Random rnd; // for several randomizations

    public CatClusterer(int numClusters, string[][] rawData)
    {
      this.numClusters = numClusters;
      MakeDataMatrix(rawData); // convert strings to ints into this.dataAsInts[][]
      Allocate(); // allocate all arrays & matrices (no initialize values)
    }

    public int[] Cluster(int numRestarts, out double catUtility)
    {
      // restart version
      int numRows = dataAsInts.Length;
      double currCU, bestCU = 0.0;
      int[] bestClustering = new int[numRows];
      for (int start = 0; start < numRestarts; ++start)
      {
        int seed = start; // use the start index as rnd seed
        int[] currClustering = ClusterOnce(seed, out currCU);
```

```
      if (currCU > bestCU)
      {
        bestCU = currCU;
        Array.Copy(currClustering, bestClustering, numRows);
      }
    }
    catUtility = bestCU;
    return bestClustering;
  } // Cluster

  private int[] ClusterOnce(int seed, out double catUtility)
  {
    this.rnd = new Random(seed);
    Initialize(); // clustering[] to -1, all counts[] to 0

    int numTrials = dataAsInts.Length; // for initial tuple assignments
    int[] goodIndexes = GetGoodIndices(numTrials); // tuples that are dissimilar
    for (int k = 0; k < numClusters; ++k) // assign first tuples to clusters
      Assign(goodIndexes[k], k);

    int numRows = dataAsInts.Length;
    int[] rndSequence = new int[numRows];
    for (int i = 0; i < numRows; ++i)
      rndSequence[i] = i;
    Shuffle(rndSequence); // present tuples in random sequence

    for (int t = 0; t < numRows; ++t)  // main loop. walk through each tuple
    {
      int idx = rndSequence[t]; // index of data tuple to process
      if (clustering[idx] != -1) continue;  // tuple clustered by initialization

      double[] candidateCU = new double[numClusters];  // candidate CU values

      for (int k = 0; k < numClusters; ++k) // examine each cluster
      {
        Assign(idx, k); // tentative cluster assignment
        candidateCU[k] = CategoryUtility(); // compute and save the CU
        Unassign(idx, k); // undo tentative assignment
      }

      int bestK = MaxIndex(candidateCU);  // greedy. the index is a cluster ID
      Assign(idx, bestK); // now we know which cluster gave the best CU
    } // each tuple

    catUtility = CategoryUtility();
    int[] result = new int[numRows];
    Array.Copy(this.clustering, result, numRows);
    return result;
  } // ClusterOnce

  private void MakeDataMatrix(string[][] rawData)
  {
    int numRows = rawData.Length;
    int numCols = rawData[0].Length;

    this.dataAsInts = new int[numRows][]; // allocate all
    for (int i = 0; i < numRows; ++i)
      dataAsInts[i] = new int[numCols];
```

```csharp
  for (int col = 0; col < numCols; ++col)
  {
    int idx = 0;
    Dictionary<string, int> dict = new Dictionary<string, int>();
    for (int row = 0; row < numRows; ++row) // build dict for curr col
    {
      string s = rawData[row][col];
      if (dict.ContainsKey(s) == false)
        dict.Add(s, idx++);
    }
    for (int row = 0; row < numRows; ++row) // use dict
    {
      string s = rawData[row][col];
      int v = dict[s];
      this.dataAsInts[row][col] = v;
    }
  }
  return; // explicit return style
}

private void Allocate()
{
  // assumes dataAsInts has been created
  // allocate this.clustering[], this.clusterCounts[], this.valueCounts[][][]
  int numRows = dataAsInts.Length;
  int numCols = dataAsInts[0].Length;

  this.clustering = new int[numRows];
  this.clusterCounts = new int[numClusters + 1]; // last cell is sum

  this.valueCounts = new int[numCols][][]; // 1st dim

  for (int col = 0; col < numCols; ++col) // need # distinct values in each col
  {
    int maxVal = 0;
    for (int i = 0; i < numRows; ++i)
    {
      if (dataAsInts[i][col] > maxVal)
        maxVal = dataAsInts[i][col];
    }
    this.valueCounts[col] = new int[maxVal + 1][]; // 0-based 2nd dim
  }

  for (int i = 0; i < this.valueCounts.Length; ++i) // 3rd dim
    for (int j = 0; j < this.valueCounts[i].Length; ++j)
      this.valueCounts[i][j] = new int[numClusters + 1]; // +1 last cell is sum

  return;
}

private void Initialize()
{
  for (int i = 0; i < clustering.Length; ++i)
    clustering[i] = -1;

  for (int i = 0; i < clusterCounts.Length; ++i)
    clusterCounts[i] = 0;

  for (int i = 0; i < valueCounts.Length; ++i)
    for (int j = 0; j < valueCounts[i].Length; ++j)
```

```
      for (int k = 0; k < valueCounts[i][j].Length; ++k)
        valueCounts[i][j][k] = 0;

  return;
}

private double CategoryUtility() // called by ClusterOnce
{
  // because CU is called many times use precomputed counts
  int numTuplesAssigned = clusterCounts[clusterCounts.Length - 1]; // last cell

  double[] clusterProbs = new double[this.numClusters];
  for (int k = 0; k < numClusters; ++k)
    clusterProbs[k] = (clusterCounts[k] * 1.0) / numTuplesAssigned;

  // single unconditional prob term
  double unconditional = 0.0;
  for (int i = 0; i < valueCounts.Length; ++i)
  {
    for (int j = 0; j < valueCounts[i].Length; ++j)
    {
      int sum = valueCounts[i][j][numClusters]; // last cell holds sum
      double p = (sum * 1.0) / numTuplesAssigned;
      unconditional += (p * p);
    }
  }

  // conditional terms each cluster
  double[] conditionals = new double[numClusters];
  for (int k = 0; k < numClusters; ++k)
  {
    for (int i = 0; i < valueCounts.Length; ++i) // each att
    {
      for (int j = 0; j < valueCounts[i].Length; ++j) // each value
      {
        double p = (valueCounts[i][j][k] * 1.0) / clusterCounts[k];
        conditionals[k] += (p * p);
      }
    }
  }

  // we have P(Ck), EE P(Ai=Vij|Ck)^2, EE P(Ai=Vij)^2 so we can compute CU easily
  double summation = 0.0;
  for (int k = 0; k < numClusters; ++k)
    summation += clusterProbs[k] * (conditionals[k] - unconditional);
    // E P(Ck) * [ EE P(Ai=Vij|Ck)^2 - EE P(Ai=Vij)^2 ] / n

  return summation / numClusters;
} // CategoryUtility

private static int MaxIndex(double[] cus)
{
  // helper for ClusterOnce. returns index of largest value in array
  double bestCU = 0.0;
  int indexOfBestCU = 0;
  for (int k = 0; k < cus.Length; ++k)
  {
    if (cus[k] > bestCU)
    {
```

```
        bestCU = cus[k];
        indexOfBestCU = k;
      }
    }
    return indexOfBestCU;
}

private void Shuffle(int[] indices) // instance so can use class rnd
{
    for (int i = 0; i < indices.Length; ++i) // Fisher-Yates shuffle
    {
        int ri = rnd.Next(i, indices.Length); // random index
        int tmp = indices[i];
        indices[i] = indices[ri]; // swap
        indices[ri] = tmp;
    }
}

private void Assign(int dataIndex, int clusterID)
{
    // assign tuple at dataIndex to clustering[] cluster, and
    // update valueCounts[][][], clusterCounts[]
    clustering[dataIndex] = clusterID; // assign

    for (int i = 0; i < valueCounts.Length; ++i) // update valueCounts
    {
        int v = dataAsInts[dataIndex][i]; // att value
        ++valueCounts[i][v][clusterID];   // bump count
        ++valueCounts[i][v][numClusters]; // bump sum
    }
    ++clusterCounts[clusterID]; // update clusterCounts
    ++clusterCounts[numClusters]; // last cell is sum
}

private void Unassign(int dataIndex, int clusterID)
{
    clustering[dataIndex] = -1; // unassign
    for (int i = 0; i < valueCounts.Length; ++i) // update
    {
        int v = dataAsInts[dataIndex][i];
        --valueCounts[i][v][clusterID];
        --valueCounts[i][v][numClusters]; // last cell is sum
    }
    --clusterCounts[clusterID]; // update clusterCounts
    --clusterCounts[numClusters]; // last cell
}

private int[] GetGoodIndices(int numTrials)
{
    // return numClusters indices of tuples that are different
    int numRows = dataAsInts.Length;
    int numCols = dataAsInts[0].Length;
    int[] result = new int[numClusters];

    int largestDiff = -1; // differences for a set of numClusters tuples
    for (int trial = 0; trial < numTrials; ++trial)
    {
        int[] candidates = Reservoir(numClusters, numRows);
        int numDifferences = 0; // for these candidates
```

```
        for (int i = 0; i < candidates.Length - 1; ++i) // all possible pairs
        {
          for (int j = i + 1; j < candidates.Length; ++j)
          {
            int aRow = candidates[i];
            int bRow = candidates[j];

            for (int col = 0; col < numCols; ++col)
              if (dataAsInts[aRow][col] != dataAsInts[bRow][col])
                ++numDifferences;
          }
        }

        //for (int i = 0; i < candidates.Length - 1; ++i) // only adjacent pairs
        //{
        //   int aRow = candidates[i];
        //   int bRow = candidates[i+1];
        //   for (int col = 0; col < numCols; ++col)
        //     if (dataAsInts[aRow][col] != dataAsInts[bRow][col])
        //       ++numDifferences;
        //}

        if (numDifferences > largestDiff)
        {
          largestDiff = numDifferences;
          Array.Copy(candidates, result, numClusters);
        }
      } // trial
      return result;
    }

    private int[] Reservoir(int n, int range) // helper for GetGoodIndices
    {
      // select n random indices between [0, range)
      int[] result = new int[n];
      for (int i = 0; i < n; ++i)
        result[i] = i;

      for (int t = n; t < range; ++t)
      {
        int j = rnd.Next(0, t + 1);
        if (j < n)
          result[j] = t;
      }
      return result;
    }
  } // CatClusterer
} // ns
```

Chapter 3 Logistic Regression Classification

Introduction

Machine learning classification is the process of creating a software system that predicts which class a data item belongs to. For example, you might want to predict the sex (male or female) of a person based on features such as height, occupation, and spending behavior. Or you might want to predict the credit worthiness of a business (low, medium, or high) based on predictors such as annual revenue, current debt, and so on. In situations where the class to predict has just two possible values, such as sex, which can be male or female, the problem is called binary classification. In situations where the dependent class has three or more possible values, the problem is called a multiclass problem.

Machine learning vocabulary can vary wildly, but problems where the goal is to predict some numeric value, as opposed to predicting a class, are often called regression problems. For example, you might want to predict the number of points some football team will score based on predictors such as opponent, home field advantage factor, average number of points scored in previous games, and so on. This is a regression problem.

There are many different machine learning approaches to classification. Examples include naive Bayes classification, probit classification, neural network classification, and decision tree classification. Perhaps the most common type of classification technique is called logistic regression classification. In spite of the fact that logistic regression classification contains the word "regression", it is really a classification technique, not a regression technique. Adding to the confusion is the fact that logistic regression classification is usually shortened to "logistic regression," rather than the more descriptive "logistic classification."

The best way to get an understanding of logistic regression classification is to examine the screenshot in **Figure 3-a**. The goal of the demo program is to predict whether a hospital patient will die or not based on three predictors: age, sex, and the result of a kidney test. Because the class to predict has just two possible values, die or survive, the demo is a binary classification problem.

All classification techniques use the same general approach. They rely on a set of data with known input and output values to create some mathematical equation that predicts the value of the dependent variable based on the independent, or predictor, variables. Then, after the model has been created, it can be used to predict the result for new data items with unknown outputs.

The demo starts with 30 (artificial) data items. The first two items are:

```
48.00   1  4.40  0
60.00  -1  7.89  1
```

The dependent variable to predict, Died, is in the last column and is encoded so that 0 represents false, meaning the person survived, and 1 represents true, meaning the person died. For the feature variables, male is encoded as -1 and female is encoded as +1. The first line of data means a 48-year-old female, with a kidney test score of 4.40 survived. The second data item indicates that there was a 60-year-old male with a 7.89 kidney score who died.

```
file:///F:/Data/MachineLearningSuccinctly/Code/Chapter3/Logisti...

Begin Logistic Regression Binary Classification demo
Goal is to predict death (0 = false, 1 = true)

Raw data:

            Age         Sex        Kidney     Died
     ===============================================
[  0]     48.00        1.00        4.40       0.00
[  1]     60.00       -1.00        7.89       1.00
[  2]     51.00       -1.00        3.48       0.00
[  3]     66.00       -1.00        8.41       1.00
[  4]     40.00        1.00        3.05       0.00
. . .
[29]      68.00       -1.00        8.38       1.00

Normalizing age and kidney data
Done

Normalized data:

[  0]     -0.74        1.00       -0.61       0.00
[  1]      0.19       -1.00        1.36       1.00
[  2]     -0.51       -1.00       -1.12       0.00
[  3]      0.66       -1.00        1.65       1.00
[  4]     -1.36        1.00       -1.37       0.00
. . .
[29]       0.82       -1.00        1.63       1.00

Creating train (80%) and test (20%) matrices
Done

Normalized training data:

[  0]     -0.43        1.00       -0.99       0.00
[  1]     -0.51       -1.00        0.26       0.00
[  2]      1.44       -1.00        1.31       1.00
. . .
[23]      -0.58       -1.00        0.52       0.00

Creating LR binary classifier
Setting maxEpochs = 100
Starting training using simplex optimization
Training complete

Best weights found:
-4.4180 0.2797 -0.5291 4.5158

Prediction accuracy on training data = 0.9583
Prediction accuracy on test data = 0.8333

End LR binary classification demo
```

Figure 3-a: Logistic Regression Binary Classification

After reading the data set into memory, the demo program normalizes the independent variables (sometimes called x-data) of age and kidney score. This means that the values are scaled to have roughly the same magnitude so that ages, which have relatively large magnitudes like 55.0 and 68.0, won't overwhelm kidney scores that have smaller magnitudes like 3.85 and 6.33. After normalization, the first two data items are now:

```
-0.74   1  -0.61  0
 0.19  -1   1.36  1
```

For normalized data, values less than zero indicate below average, and values greater than zero indicate above average. So for the first data item, the age (-0.74) is below average, and the kidney score (-0.61) is also below average. For the second data item, both age (+0.19) and kidney score (+1.36) are above average.

After normalizing the 30-item source data set, the demo program divides the set into two parts: a training set, which consists of 80% of the items (24 items) and a test set, which has the remaining 20% (6 items). The split process is done in a way so that data items are randomly assigned to either the training or test sets. The training data is used to create the prediction model, and the test data is used after the model has been created to get an estimate of how accurate the model will be when presented with new data that has unknown output values.

After the training and test sets are generated, the demo creates a prediction model using logistic regression classification. When using logistic regression classification (or any other kind of classification), there are several techniques that can be used to find values for the weights that define the model. The demo program uses a technique called simplex optimization.

The result of the training process is four weights with the values { -4.41, 0.27, -0.52, and 4.51 }. As you'll see later, the second weight value, 0.27, is associated with the age predictor, the third weight value, -0.52, is associated with the sex predictor, and the last weight value, 4.51, is associated with the kidney score predictor. The first weight value, -4.41, is a constant needed by the model, but is not directly associated with any one specific predictor variable.

After the logistic regression classification model is created, the demo program applies the model to the training and test data, and computes the predictive accuracy of the model. The model correctly predicts 95.83% of the training data (which is 23 out of 24 correct) and 83.33% of the test data (5 out of 6 correct). The 83.33% can be interpreted as an estimate of how accurate the model will be when presented with new, previously unseen data.

Understanding Logistic Regression Classification

Suppose some raw age, sex, and kidney data is { 50.0, -1, 6.0 }, which represents a 50-year-old male with a kidney score of 6.0. Here, the data is not normalized to keep the ideas clear. Now suppose you have four weights: $b_0 = -7.50$, $b_1 = 0.11$, $b_2 = -0.22$, and $b_3 = 0.33$. One possible way to create a simple linear model would be like so:

$$Y = b_0 + b_1(50.0) + b_2(-1) + b_3(6.0)$$
$$= -7.50 + (0.11)(50.0) + (-0.22)(-1) + (0.33)(6.0)$$
$$= 0.20$$

In other words, you'd multiply each input x-value by an associated weight value, sum those products, and add a constant. Logistic regression classification extends this idea by using a more complex math equation that requires a pair of calculations:

$Z = b_0 + b_1(50.0) + b_2(-1) + b_3(6.0)$
$Y = 1.0 / (1.0 + e^{-Z})$

In other words, for logistic regression classification, you form a linear combination of weights and inputs, call that sum Z, and then feed that result to a second equation that involves the math constant e. The constant e is just a number with value 2.7182818, and it appears in many math equations, in many different fields.

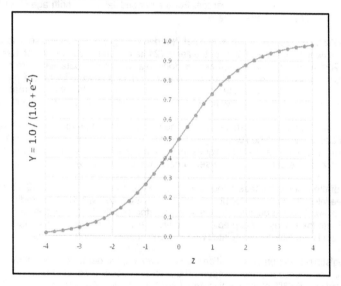

Figure 3-b: The Logistic Sigmoid Function

The function $Y = 1.0 / (1.0 + e^{-Z})$ has many important uses in machine learning, and forms the basis of logistic regression classification. The function is called the logistic sigmoid function, or sometimes the log sigmoid, or just the sigmoid function for short. The logistic sigmoid function can accept any Z-value from negative infinity to positive infinity, but the output is always a value between 0 and 1, as shown in **Figure 3-b**.

This may be mildly interesting, but what's the point? The idea is that if you have some input x-values and associated weights (often called the b-values) and you combine them, and then feed the sum, Z, to the logistic sigmoid function, then the result will be between 0 and 1. This result is the predicted output value.

An example will clarify. As before, suppose that for a hospital patient, some un-normalized age, sex, and kidney x-values are { 50.0, -1, 6.0 }, and suppose the b-weights are $b_0 = -7.50$, $b_1 = 0.11$, $b_2 = -0.22$, and $b_3 = 0.33$. And assume that class 0 is "die is false" and class 1 is "die is true".

The logistic regression calculation goes like so:

$Z = b_0 + b_1(50.0) + b_2(-1) + b_3(6.0)$
   $= 0.20$

$Y = 1.0 / (1.0 + e^{-Z})$
   $= 1.0 / (1.0 + e^{-0.20})$
   $= 0.5498$

The final predicted output value (0 or 1) is the one closest to the computed output value. Because 0.5498 is closer to 1 than to 0, you'd conclude that dependent variable "died" is true. But if the y-value had been 0.3333 for example, because that value is closer to 0 than to 1, you'd conclude "died" is false. An equivalent, but slightly less obvious, interpretation is that the computed output value is the probability of the 1-class.

Now if you have many training data items with known results, you can compute the accuracy of your model-weights. So the problem now becomes, how do you find the best set of weight values? The process of finding the set of weight values so that computed output values closely match the known output values for some set of training data is called training the model. There are roughly a dozen major techniques that can be used to train a logistic regression classification model. These include techniques such as simple gradient descent, back-propagation, particle swarm optimization, and Newton-Raphson. The demo program uses a technique called simplex optimization.

Demo Program Overall Structure

To create the demo, I launched Visual Studio and selected the new C# console application template. The demo has no significant .NET version dependencies so any version of Visual Studio should work.

After the template code loaded into the editor, I removed all using statements at the top of the source code, except for the single reference to the top-level System namespace. In the Solution Explorer window, I renamed file Program.cs to the more descriptive LogisticProgram.cs and Visual Studio automatically renamed class Program to LogisticProgram.

The overall structure of the demo program, with a few minor edits to save space, is presented in **Listing 3-a**. The complete program source code is at the end of this chapter. In order to keep the size of the example code small, and the main ideas as clear as possible, the demo program omits normal error checking that would be used in production code.

```
using System;
namespace LogisticRegression
{
  class LogisticProgram
  {
    static void Main(string[] args)
    {
      Console.WriteLine("Begin Logistic Regression Binary Classification demo");

      double[][] data = new double[30][];
      data[0] = new double[] { 48, +1, 4.40, 0 };
```

```
      data[1] = new double[] { 60, -1, 7.89, 1 };
      . . .
      data[29] = new double[] { 68, -1, 8.38, 1 };

      Console.WriteLine("Raw data: ");
      ShowData(data, 5, 2, true);

      Console.WriteLine("Normalizing age and kidney data");
      int[] columns = new int[] { 0, 2 };
      double[][] means = Normalize(data, columns);

      Console.WriteLine("Normalized data: ");
      ShowData(data, 5, 2, true);

      Console.WriteLine("Creating train (80%) and test (20%) matrices");
      double[][] trainData;
      double[][] testData;
      MakeTrainTest(data, 0, out trainData, out testData);

      Console.WriteLine("Normalized training data: ");
      ShowData(trainData, 3, 2, true);

      int numFeatures = 3;
      LogisticClassifier lc = new LogisticClassifier(numFeatures);
      int maxEpochs = 100;
      double[] bestWeights = lc.Train(trainData, maxEpochs, 33);

      Console.WriteLine("Best weights found:");
      ShowVector(bestWeights, 4, true);

      double trainAccuracy = lc.Accuracy(trainData, bestWeights);
      Console.WriteLine("Prediction accuracy on training data = " +
        trainAccuracy.ToString("F4"));

      double testAccuracy = lc.Accuracy(testData, bestWeights);
      Console.WriteLine("Prediction accuracy on test data = " +
        testAccuracy.ToString("F4"));

      Console.WriteLine("End LR binary classification demo");
      Console.ReadLine();
    } // Main

    static double[][] Normalize(double[][] rawData,
      int[] columns) { . . }
    static void Normalize(double[][] rawData, int[] columns,
      double[][] means) { . . }
    static void MakeTrainTest(double[][] allData, int seed,
      out double[][] trainData, out double[][] testData) { . . }
    static void ShowData(double[][] data, int numRows,
      int decimals, bool indices) { . . }
  } // Program

  public class LogisticClassifier { . . }
}
```

Listing 3-a: Logistic Regression Classification Demo Program Structure

The demo program class has four static helper methods, including two different Normalize methods. The first Normalize method normalizes the specified columns of a matrix of data and returns the mean and standard deviation of each column. This will be explained later.

The second Normalize method scales the specified columns of a data matrix using supplied means and standard deviations that were presumably computed earlier by the first overloaded Normalize method. Helper method MakeTrainTest accepts a data matrix and returns a random 80% of the data into a training matrix (as an out-parameter) and the remaining 20% of the data into a test matrix (as a second out-parameter). Helper method ShowData displays the values in a data matrix to the console shell.

All the classification logic is contained in a single program-defined class named LogisticRegression. All the program logic is contained in the Main method. The Main method begins by setting up 30 hard-coded data items (age, sex, kidney score, death) in an array-of-arrays style matrix:

```
static void Main(string[] args)
{
  Console.WriteLine("\nBegin Logistic Regression Binary Classification demo");
  double[][] data = new double[30][];
  data[0] = new double[] { 48, +1, 4.40, 0 };
  data[1] = new double[] { 60, -1, 7.89, 1 };
. . .
```

In a non-demo scenario, you would likely have data stored in a text file and would load the data into memory using a helper function. Next, the data is displayed:

```
Console.WriteLine("\nRaw data: \n");
Console.WriteLine("      Age      Sex      Kidney   Died");
Console.WriteLine("===================================");
ShowData(data, 5, 2, true);
```

Because the data has been stored directly into a numeric matrix, there is no column header information available as there likely would be if the data were in a text file, so a crude, hard-coded header is displayed directly. Next, the data set is normalized and displayed:

```
Console.WriteLine("Normalizing age and kidney data");
int[] columns = new int[] { 0, 2 };
double[][] means = Normalize(data, columns);
Console.WriteLine("Done");
Console.WriteLine("\nNormalized data: \n");
ShowData(data, 5, 2, true);
```

The Normalize method will be explained in detail in the next section. Next, the data set is split into a training matrix and a test matrix:

```
Console.WriteLine("Creating train (80%) and test (20%) matrices");
double[][] trainData;
double[][] testData;
MakeTrainTest(data, 0, out trainData, out testData);
Console.WriteLine("Done");
Console.WriteLine("\nNormalized training data: \n");
ShowData(trainData, 3, 2, true);
```

Notice that the 80-20 percentage split is hard-coded. A more flexible alternative is to parameterize the split percentage.

The logistic regression classification is encapsulated in an object that is instantiated like so:

```
int numFeatures = 3;
Console.WriteLine("Creating LR binary classifier");
LogisticClassifier lc = new LogisticClassifier(numFeatures);
```

The program-defined LogisticClassifier object requires just a single parameter for the constructor: the number of features. For the demo, this is 3, for age, sex, and kidney score. Next, the classifier is trained:

```
int maxEpochs = 100;
Console.WriteLine("Setting maxEpochs = " + maxEpochs);
Console.WriteLine("Starting training using simplex optimization");
double[] bestWeights = lc.Train(trainData, maxEpochs, 33);
Console.WriteLine("Training complete");
Console.WriteLine("\nBest weights found:");
ShowVector(bestWeights, 4, true);
```

Most classification training is iterative, and it is surprisingly difficult to know when to stop the training process. Here, variable maxEpochs sets a limit on the main processing loop. The value of 100 is artificially small to give a representative demo. The argument of 33 passed to the Train method is a seed for a random number generator, which is used by the method, as you'll see shortly. The value 33 was used only because it gave a representative demo.

Method Main concludes by computing the model's classification accuracy:

```
. . .
  double trainAccuracy = lc.Accuracy(trainData, bestWeights);
  Console.WriteLine("Prediction accuracy on training data = " +
    trainAccuracy.ToString("F4"));

  double testAccuracy = lc.Accuracy(testData, bestWeights);
  Console.WriteLine("Prediction accuracy on test data = " +
    testAccuracy.ToString("F4"));

  Console.WriteLine("\nEnd LR binary classification demo\n");
  Console.ReadLine();
}
```

Notice the demo does not perform any predictions using the final model. In order to make predictions using a model that was trained using normalized data, you must use normalized data. I'll present an example of this in the next section. Additionally, the demo does not save the model, because that also would require normalization information.

Data Normalization

In theory, when performing logistic regression classification, it's not necessary to normalize your data. But in practice normalization usually helps to create a good prediction model. There are two main types of normalization, called Gaussian and min-max. The demo uses Gaussian normalization, sometimes called z-score normalization (where z is not the same as the intermediate logistic regression Z value in the previous section).

The motivation for data normalization is simple. You want to deal with situations where some data items have much larger magnitudes than others. For example, imagine data where one feature is a person's annual income, with values like 56,000.00, and another feature is the person's number of children, with values like 2.0. Without normalization, when computing the intermediate Z value, the contribution of the income value would be much larger than the contribution of the children value.

Gaussian normalization of the values in some column of data replaces each raw value x with (x - m) / sd, where m is the column mean and sd is the column standard deviation. Suppose a feature is a person's age and there are just four values: { 25, 36, 40, 23 }. The mean (average) of the values is:

m = (25 + 36 + 40 + 23) / 4
= 124 / 4
= 31.0

The standard deviation is the square root of the average of squared differences between values and the mean:

sd = sqrt(($(25 - 31.0)^2$ + $(36 - 31.0)^2$ + $(40 - 31.0)^2$ + $(23 - 31.0)^2$) / 4)
= sqrt((36.0 + 25.0 + 81.0 + 64.0) / 4)
= sqrt(51.5)
= 7.176

So the normalized value for the first age, 25, is: (25 - 31.0) / 7.176 = -0.84. After normalization, in general, all values will be between about -10.0 and +10.0, and in most cases will be between -4.0 and +4.0. Any value that is not in this range is extreme and should be investigated.

The demo program has two Normalize methods. The first method accepts a matrix of data, and an array of columns to normalize. The method normalizes the matrix in place, and returns the mean and standard deviations of each column in a mini-matrix. The idea is that this information may be needed later if you want to make predictions about new data, so that the new data can be normalized using the same information that was used to create the prediction model.

The code for method Normalize begins:

```
static double[][] Normalize(double[][] rawData, int[] columns)
{
  int numRows = rawData.Length;
  int numCols = rawData[0].Length;
  double[][] result = new double[2][];
  for (int i = 0; i < 2; ++i)
    result[i] = new double[numCols];
. . .
```

The local matrix result will hold the means and standard deviations used during normalization. That mini-matrix has 2 rows, where the first row holds column means, and the second row holds column standard deviations. For example, the return result for the demo data is:

```
57.50  -0.13  5.48  0.33
12.84   0.99  1.78  0.47
```

This indicates the mean of column 0 (age) is 57.50, the mean of column 1 (sex) is -0.13, the mean of column 2 (kidney score) is 5.48, and the mean of column 3, the dependent variable "died", is 0.33. The second row values are the standard deviations, so the standard deviation of column 0, age, is 12.84, and so on.

Notice that means and standard deviations are computed for all columns. An alternative is to compute means and standard deviations just for the specified columns, leaving 0.0 values in non-normalized columns.

After setting up the return matrix, method Normalize computes and saves the mean of each column by adding up all column values and dividing by the number of items in the column:

```
for (int c = 0; c < numCols; ++c)
{
  double sum = 0.0;
  for (int r = 0; r < numRows; ++r)
    sum += rawData[r][c];
  double mean = sum / numRows;
  result[0][c] = mean; // save
. . .
```

After means have been computed, they can be used to compute the standard deviations:

```
. . .
  double sumSquares = 0.0;
  for (int r = 0; r < numRows; ++r)
    sumSquares += (rawData[r][c] - mean) * (rawData[r][c] - mean);
  double stdDev = Math.Sqrt(sumSquares / numRows);
  result[1][c] = stdDev;
} // for
```

Method Normalize finishes by performing the Gaussian normalization on the specified columns and returning the means and standard deviations mini-matrix result:

```
. . .
  for (int c = 0; c < columns.Length; ++c)
  {
    int j = columns[c]; // column to normalize
    double mean = result[0][j];
    double stdDev = result[1][j];
    for (int i = 0; i < numRows; ++i)
      rawData[i][j] = (rawData[i][j] - mean) / stdDev;
  }
  return result;
}
```

Notice the Normalize method modifies its input matrix. An alternative would be to return normalized values in a new matrix. There are two minor downsides to this approach. First, you'd need twice as much memory because you'd be storing two data matrices instead of just one. Second, you'd be returning two matrices, the normalized data and the means and standard deviations mini-matrix, so you'd have to resort to using out-parameters.

Remember, the demo program does not do any predictions. Suppose you have a new patient whose age is 58, sex is male, and kidney score is 7.00. A prediction for this data item could look like:

```
int[] columns = new int[] { 0, 2 };
double[][] means = Normalize(data, columns);
. . .
double[][] unknown = new double[1][];
unknown[0] = new double[] { 58.0, -1.0, 7.00 };
Normalize(unknown, columns, means);
int died = lc.ComputeDependent(unknown[0], bestWeights);
Console.WriteLine("Died = " + died);
```

First, a one-row matrix named "unknown" is created with the relevant x-data. Notice there is no value for the "died" dependent variable. The x-data cannot be used as-is because the logistic regression model is expecting normalized data, not raw data. So the new data matrix is passed to the overloaded Normalize method, along with the computed means and standard deviation matrix, to generate normalized new data. This data is fed to a ComputeDependent method (which will be explained later) along with the weights found during training.

The calling code is a bit clunky. An alternative is to wrap the code in a method named something like "Predict" that could be called like this:

```
double[] unknown = new double[] { 58.0, -1.0, 7.00 };
int died = Predict(unknown, columns, means, bestWeights);
```

When writing custom machine learning code, there's often a tradeoff between keeping the number of helper methods small (but requiring somewhat awkward calling code) and writing numerous easy-to-call helpers (but requiring a lot more code).

Creating Training and Test Data

One approach to creating a logistic regression classification model is to simply train the model using all available data. However, it's better in most situations to hold out some of the data so that the model can be evaluated to give an estimate of its accuracy when presented with new, previously unseen data.

As it turns out, if you train long enough, it's almost always possible to create a model that predicts perfectly or nearly perfectly, but the model will typically fail miserably when presented with new data. This problem is called model over-fitting. Holding out some test data can help avoid over-fitting; even if you create a model that has 100% accuracy on training data, if the model has poor accuracy on the test data, it's almost certainly not a good predictive model, and so you need to revise the model.

Helper method MakeTrainTest is conceptually simple, but it involves some fairly subtle programming techniques. Imagine you have some data named "allData", with nine rows and four columns, stored in an array-of-arrays style matrix, as shown in the left part of **Figure 3-c**. The first step is to make a copy of the matrix. Although you could create a replica of the source matrix values, a more efficient approach is to make a copy by reference.

The reference copy is named "copy" in the figure. Note that for clarity, although the arrows in the cells of matrix copy are shown pointing to the arrow-cells in matrix allData, the arrows in copy are really pointing to the data cells in allData. For example, the arrow in copy[0][] is shown pointing to cell allData[0][] when in fact it should be pointing to the cell containing the 5.3 value.

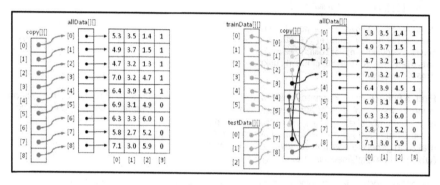

Figure 3-c: Creating Training and Test Matrices by Reference

After creating a reference copy, the next step is to scramble the order of the copy. This is shown on the right. After scrambling, the last step is to create training and test matrices by reference. In **Figure 3-c**, the first row of training data points to the first cell in the copy, which in turn points to the second row of the data. In other words, trainData[0][0] is 4.9, trainData[0][1] is 3.7, and so on. Similarly, testData[0][0] is 6.4, testData[0][1] is 3.9 and so on.

The definition of method MakeTrainTest begins with:

```
static void MakeTrainTest(double[][] allData, int seed,
      out double[][] trainData, out double[][] testData)
{
  Random rnd = new Random(seed);
  int totRows = allData.Length;
  int numTrainRows = (int)(totRows * 0.80);
  int numTestRows = totRows - numTrainRows;
. . .
```

The local Random object will be used to scramble row order. It accepts a seed parameter, so you can generate different results by passing in a different seed value. Here, for simplicity, the percentage split is hard-coded as 80-20. A more flexible approach is to pass the train percentage as a parameter, being careful to handle 0.80 versus 80.0 values for 80 percent.

The reference copy is made:

```
double[][] copy = new double[allData.Length][];
for (int i = 0; i < copy.Length; ++i)
  copy[i] = allData[i];
```

When working with references, even simple code can be tricky. For example, `allData[0][0]` is a cell value, like 4.5, but `allData[0]` is a reference to the first row of data.

Next, the rows of the copy matrix are scrambled, also by reference:

```
for (int i = 0; i < copy.Length; ++i)
{
  int r = rnd.Next(i, copy.Length);
  double[] tmp = copy[r];
  copy[r] = copy[i];
  copy[i] = tmp;
}
```

The scramble code uses the clever Fisher-Yates mini-algorithm. The net result is that the references in the copy matrix will be reordered randomly as suggested by the colored arrows in **Figure 3-c**. Method MakeTrainTest finishes by assigning the first 80% of scrambled rows in the copy matrix to the training out-matrix and the remaining rows to the test out-matrix:

```
. . .
  for (int i = 0; i < numTrainRows; ++i)
    trainData[i] = copy[i];

  for (int i = 0; i < numTestRows; ++i)
    testData[i] = copy[i + numTrainRows];
}
```

Defining the LogisticClassifier Class

The structure of the program-defined LogisticClassifier class is presented in **Listing 3-b**. The class has three data members. Variable numFeatures holds the number of predictor variables for a problem. Array weights holds the values used to compute outputs.

```
public class LogisticClassifier
{
  private int numFeatures;
  private double[] weights;
  private Random rnd;

  public LogisticClassifier(int numFeatures) { . . }
  public double[] Train(double[][] trainData, int maxEpochs, int seed) { . . }

  private double[] ReflectedWts(double[] centroidWts, double[] worstWts) { . . }
  private double[] ExpandedWts(double[] centroidWts, double[] worstWts) { . . }
  private double[] ContractedWts(double[] centroidWts, double[] worstWts) { . . }
  private double[] RandomSolutionWts() { . . }
  private double Error(double[][] trainData, double[] weights) { . . }
```

```
public double ComputeOutput(double[] dataItem, double[] weights) { . . }
public int ComputeDependent(double[] dataItem, double[] weights) { . . }
public double Accuracy(double[][] trainData, double[] weights) { . . }

private class Solution : IComparable<Solution> { . . }
}
```

Listing 3-b: The LogisticClassifier Class

Class member rnd is a Random object that is used during the training process to generate random possible solutions.

The class exposes a single constructor and four public methods. Method Train uses a technique called simplex optimization to find values for the weights array, so that computed output values closely match the known output values in the training data.

Method ComputeOutput accepts some x-data and a set of weight values and returns a raw value between 0.0 and 1.0. This output is used by the training method to compute error. Method ComputeDependent is similar to method ComputeOutput, except that it returns a 0 or 1 result. This output is used to compute accuracy. Public method Accuracy accepts a set of weights and a matrix of either training data or test data, and returns the percentage of correct predictions.

There are five private methods: Error, RandomSolutionWts, ReflectedWts, ExpandedWts, and ContractedWts. All of these methods are used by method Train when searching for the best set of weight values.

The LogisticClassifier contains a nested private class named Solution. This class is used during training to define potential solutions, that is, potential best sets of weight values. The Solution class could have been defined outside the LogisticClassifier class, but you can define Solution as a nested class for a slightly cleaner design.

The LogisticClassifier constructor is very simple:

```
public LogisticClassifier(int numFeatures)
{
  this.numFeatures = numFeatures; // number predictors
  this.weights = new double[numFeatures + 1]; // [0] = b0 constant
}
```

If you review how the logistic regression calculation works, you'll see that the number of weight b-values has to be one more than the number of feature x-values because each x-value has an associated weight and there is one additional weight for the b_0 constant. An alternative design is to store the b_0 value in a separate variable.

Method ComputeOutput is simple, but does have one subtle point. The method is defined:

```
public double ComputeOutput(double[] dataItem, double[] weights)
{
  double z = 0.0;
  z += weights[0]; // b0 constant
  for (int i = 0; i < weights.Length - 1; ++i) // data might include Y
```

```
    z += (weights[i + 1] * dataItem[i]); // skip first weight
    return 1.0 / (1.0 + Math.Exp(-z));
}
```

For flexibility, the method accepts an array parameter named dataItem, which can represent a row of training data or test data, including a Y-value in the last cell. However, the Y-value is not used to compute output.

Method ComputeDependent is defined:

```
public int ComputeDependent(double[] dataItem, double[] weights)
{
    double sum = ComputeOutput(dataItem, weights);
    if (sum <= 0.5)
        return 0;
    else
        return 1;
}
```

Here, instead of returning a raw output value, for example 0.5678, the method returns the corresponding Y-value, which is either 0 or 1. The choice of <= instead of < is arbitrary, and has no significant effect on the operation of the classifier. A design alternative is to return a third value indicating the decision is too close to call:

```
if (sum <= 0.45)
    return 0;
else if (sum >= 0.45)
    return 1;
else
    return -1; // undecided
```

Using this alternative would require quite a few changes to the demo program code logic.

Error and Accuracy

The ultimate goal of a prediction model is accuracy, which is the percentage of correct predictions made divided by the total number of predictions made. But when searching for the best set of weight values, it is better to use a measure of error rather than accuracy. Suppose some set of weights yields these results for five training items:

```
Training Y   Computed Output   Computed Y   Result
------------------------------------------------------
    0            0.4980             0        correct
    1            0.5003             1        correct
    0            0.9905             1        wrong
    1            0.5009             1        correct
    0            0.4933             0        correct
```

The model is correct on four of the five items for an accuracy of 80%. But on the four correct predictions, the output is just barely correct, meaning output is just barely under 0.5 when giving a 0 for Y and just barely above 0.5 when giving a 1 for Y. And on the third training item, which is incorrectly predicted, the computed output of 0.9905 is not close at all to the desired output of 0.00. Now suppose a second set of weights yields these results:

```
Training Y   Computed Output   Computed Y   Result
-----------------------------------------------------
    0           0.0008            0          correct
    1           0.9875            1          correct
    0           0.5003            1          wrong
    1           0.9909            1          correct
    0           0.5105            0          wrong
```

These weights are correct on three out of five for an accuracy of 60%, which is less than the 80% of the first weights, but the three correct predictions are "very correct" (computed Y is close to 0.00 or 1.00) and the two wrong predictions are just barely wrong. In short, when training, predictive accuracy is too coarse, so using error is better.

The definition of method Accuracy begins:

```
public double Accuracy(double[][] trainData, double[] weights)
{
  int numCorrect = 0;
  int numWrong = 0;
  int yIndex = trainData[0].Length - 1;
. . .
```

Counters for the number of correct and wrong predictions are initialized, and the index in a row of training data where the dependent y-value is located is specified. This is the last column. The term trainData[0] is the first row of data, but because all rows of data are assumed to be the same, any row could have been used. Each row of data in the demo has four items, so the value of Length - 1 will be 3, which is the index of the last column. Next, the training data is examined, and its accuracy is computed and then returned:

```
. . .
  for (int i = 0; i < trainData.Length; ++i)
  {
    double computed = ComputeDependent(trainData[i], weights);
    double desired = trainData[i][yIndex]; // 0.0 or 1.0
    if (computed == desired)
      ++numCorrect;
    else
      ++numWrong;
  }
  return (numCorrect * 1.0) / (numWrong + numCorrect);
}
```

Notice that local variable computed is declared as type double, even though method ComputeDependent returns an integer 0 or 1. So an implicit conversion from 0 or 1, to 0.0 or 1.0 is performed. Therefore the condition computed == desired is comparing two values of type double for exact equality, which can be risky. However, the overhead of comparing the two values for "very-closeness" rather than exact equality is usually not worth the performance price:

```
double closeness = 0.00000001; // often called 'epsilon' in ML
if (Math.Abs(computed - desired) < closeness)
  ++numCorrect;
else
  ++numWrong;
```

The ability to control when and if to take shortcuts like this to improve performance is a major advantage of writing custom machine learning code, compared to using an existing system written by someone else where you don't have access to source code.

Method Error is very similar to method Accuracy:

```
private double Error(double[][] trainData, double[] weights)
{
  int yIndex = trainData[0].Length - 1;
  double sumSquaredError = 0.0;
  for (int i = 0; i < trainData.Length; ++i)
  {
    double computed = ComputeOutput(trainData[i], weights);
    double desired = trainData[i][yIndex]; // ex: 0.0 or 1.0
    sumSquaredError += (computed - desired) * (computed - desired);
  }
  return sumSquaredError / trainData.Length;
}
```

Method Error computes the mean squared error (sometimes called mean square error), which is abbreviated MSE in machine learning literature. Suppose there are just three training data items that yield these results:

```
Training Y    Computed Output
----------------------------
    0           0.3000
    1           0.8000
    0           0.1000
```

The sum of squared errors is:

$$sse = (0 - 0.3000)^2 + (1 - 0.8000)^2 + (0 - 0.1000)^2$$
$$= 0.09 + 0.04 + 0.01$$
$$= 0.14$$

And the mean squared error is:

$$MSE = 0.14 / 3$$
$$= 0.4667$$

A minor alternative is to use root mean squared error (RMSE), which is just the square root of the MSE.

Understanding Simplex Optimization

The most difficult technical challenge of any classification system is implementing the training sub-system. Recall that there are roughly a dozen major approaches with names like simple gradient descent, Newton-Raphson, back-propagation, and L-BFGS. All of these algorithms are fairly complex. The demo program uses a technique called simplex optimization.

Loosely speaking, a simplex is a triangle. The idea behind simplex optimization is to start with three possible solutions. One possible solution will be "best" (meaning smallest error), one will be "worst" (largest error), and the third is called "other". Next, simplex optimization creates three new possible solutions called "expanded", "reflected", and "contracted". Each of these is compared against the current worst solution, and if any of the new candidates is better (smaller error) than the current worst, the worst solution is replaced.

Expressed in very high-level pseudo-code, simplex optimization is:

```
create best, worst, other possible solutions
loop until done
  create expanded, reflected, contracted candidate replacements
  if any are better than worst, replace worst
  else if none are better, adjust worst and other solutions
end loop
```

Simplex optimization is illustrated in **Figure 3-d**. In a simple case where a solution consists of two values, like (1.23, 4.56), you can think of a solution as a point on the (x, y) plane. The left side of **Figure 3-d** shows how three new candidate solutions are generated from the current best, worst, and "other" solutions.

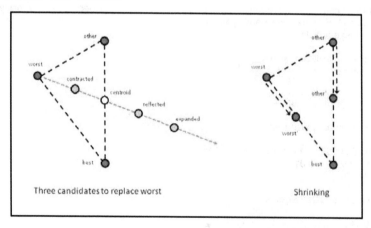

Figure 3-d: Simplex Optimization

First, a centroid is computed. The centroid is the average of the best and "other" solutions. In two dimensions, this is a point half-way between the "other" and best points. Next, an imaginary line is created, which starts at the worst point and extends through the centroid. Now, the contracted candidate is between the worst and centroid points. The reflected candidate is on the imaginary line, past the centroid. And the expanded candidate is past the reflected point.

In each iteration of simplex optimization, if one of the expanded, reflected, or contracted candidates is better than the current worst solution, worst is replaced by that candidate. If none of the three candidates generated are better than the worst solution, the current worst and "other" solutions are moved toward the best solution to points somewhere between their current position and the best solution, as shown in the right-hand side of **Figure 3-d**.

After each iteration, a new virtual "best-other-worst" triangle is formed, getting closer and closer to an optimal solution. If a snapshot of each triangle is taken, when looked at sequentially, the moving triangles resemble a pointy blob moving across the plane in a way that resembles a single-celled amoeba. For this reason, simplex optimization is sometimes called amoeba method optimization.

There are many variations of simplex optimization, which vary in how far the contracted, reflected, and expanded candidate solutions are from the current centroid, and the order in which the candidate solutions are checked to see if each is better than the current worst solution. The most common variation of simplex optimization is called the Nelder-Mead algorithm. The demo program uses a simpler variation that does not have a specific name.

In pseudo-code, the variation of simplex optimization used in the demo program is:

```
randomly initialize best, worst, other solutions
loop maxEpochs times
  create centroid from worst and other
  create expanded
  if expanded is better than worst, replace worst with expanded,
    continue loop
  create reflected
  if reflected is better than worst, replace worst with reflected,
    continue loop
  create contracted
  if contracted is better than worst, replace worst with contracted,
    continue loop
  create a random solution
  if random solution is better than worst, replace worst,
    continue loop
  shrink worst and other toward best
end loop
return best solution found
```

Simplex optimization, like all other machine learning optimization algorithms, has pros and cons. This is why there are so many different optimization techniques, each with dozens of variations. In real-life scenarios, somewhat surprisingly, no machine learning optimization technique guarantees you will find the optimal solution, if one exists. However, simplex optimization is relatively simple to implement and usually, but not always, works well in practice.

Training

The goal of the logistic regression classifier training process is to find a set of weight values so that when presented with training data, the computed output values closely match the known output values. In other words, the goal of training is to minimize the error between computed output values and known output values. This is called a numerical optimization problem because you want to optimize weight values to minimize error.

Class method Train uses a local class named Solution as part of the simplex optimization. A solution represents a possible solution to the problem of finding the weight values that minimize error. A Solution object is a collection of weights and the mean squared error associated with those weights. The definition is presented in **Listing 3-c.**

```
private class Solution : IComparable<Solution>
{
  public double[] weights;
  public double error;

  public Solution(int numFeatures)
  {
    this.weights = new double[numFeatures + 1];
    this.error = 0.0;
  }

  public int CompareTo(Solution other) // low-to-high error
  {
    if (this.error < other.error)
      return -1;
    else if (this.error > other.error)
      return 1;
    else
      return 0;
  }
}
```

Listing 3-c: The Solution Helper Class Definition

The key concept of simplex optimization is that there is a best, worst, and "other" solution, so the three current solutions must be sorted by error, from smallest error to largest. Notice that helper class Solution derives from the IComparable interface. What his means is that a collection of Solution objects can be sorted automatically.

Using a private nested class that derives from the IComparable interface is a rather exotic approach. When programming, simple is almost always better than exotic and clever (in my opinion, anyway), but in this situation, the simplification of the code in the Train method is worth the overhead of a not-very-straightforward programming technique.

The definition of method Train begins with:

```
public double[] Train(double[][] trainData, int maxEpochs, int seed)
{
  this.rnd = new Random(seed);
  Solution[] solutions = new Solution[3]; // best, worst, other
```

```
for (int i = 0; i < 3; ++i)
{
  solutions[i] = new Solution(numFeatures);
  solutions[i].weights = RandomSolutionWts();
  solutions[i].error = Error(trainData, solutions[i].weights);
}
. . .
```

First, the class member Random object rnd is instantiated with a seed value. This instantiation is performed inside method Train rather than in the constructor, so that if you wanted, you could restart training several times, using a different seed value each time to get different results.

Next, an array of Solution objects is instantiated. The whole point of going to the trouble of creating a Solution object is so that an array of solutions can be sorted to give the best, worst, and "other". The Solution object in each cell of the solutions array is instantiated by calling the constructor, and then a helper method named RandomSolutionWts supplies the values for the weights, and method Error supplies the mean squared error.

Next, the main training loop is created:

```
int best = 0;
int other = 1;
int worst = 2;
int epoch = 0;
while (epoch < maxEpochs)
{
  ++epoch;
. . .
```

Local variables best, other, and worst are set up for clarity. For example, the expression

```
solutions[2].weights[0]
```

is the first weight value in the worst solution because Solution objects are ordered from smallest error to largest. Using the local variable instead, the expression would be:

```
solutions[worst].weights[0]
```

This is a bit more clear, and likely less error-prone. The local variable epoch is just a loop counter. Inside the main loop, the three possible solutions are sorted and the centroid is computed:

```
Array.Sort(solutions);
double[] bestWts = solutions[0].weights; // convenience only
double[] otherWts = solutions[1].weights;
double[] worstWts = solutions[2].weights;
double[] centroidWts = CentroidWts(otherWts, bestWts);
```

This is where the private Solution class shows its worth, by allowing the array of Solution objects to be sorted automatically, from smallest error to largest, simply by calling the built-in Array.Sort method. As before, for convenience and clarity, the weights arrays of the three Solution objects receive local aliases bestWts, otherWts, and worstWts. Helper method CentroidWts computes a centroid based on the weights in the current best and "other" solutions.

Next, the expanded candidate replacement for the current worst solution is created. If the expanded candidate is better than the worst solution, the worst solution is replaced:

```
double[] expandedWts = ExpandedWts(centroidWts, worstWts);
double expandedError = Error(trainData, expandedWts);
if (expandedError < solutions[worst].error)
{
  Array.Copy(expandedWts, worstWts, numFeatures + 1);
  solutions[worst].error = expandedError;
  continue;
}
```

Replacing the current worst solution requires two steps. First, the weights have to be copied from the candidate into worst, and then the error term has to be copied in. This is allowed because Solution class members weights and error were declared with public scope.

As a very general rule of thumb, using the continue statement inside a while-loop can be a bit tricky, because many statements in the loop after the continue statement are skipped. In this situation, however, using the continue statement leads to cleaner and more easily modified code than the alternative of a deeply nested if-else-if structure.

If the expanded candidate is not better than the worst solution, the reflected candidate is created and examined:

```
double[] reflectedWts = ReflectedWts(centroidWts, worstWts);
double reflectedError = Error(trainData, reflectedWts);
if (reflectedError < solutions[worst].error)
{
  Array.Copy(reflectedWts, worstWts, numFeatures + 1);
  solutions[worst].error = reflectedError;
  continue;
}
```

If the reflected candidate is not better than the worst solution, the contracted candidate is created and examined:

```
double[] contractedWts = ContractedWts(centroidWts, worstWts);
double contractedError = Error(trainData, contractedWts);
if (contractedError < solutions[worst].error)
{
  Array.Copy(contractedWts, worstWts, numFeatures + 1);
  solutions[worst].error = contractedError;
  continue;
}
```

At this point, none of the three primary candidate solutions are better than the worst solution, so a random solution is tried:

```
double[] randomSolWts = RandomSolutionWts();
double randomSolError = Error(trainData, randomSolWts);
if (randomSolError < solutions[worst].error)
{
  Array.Copy(randomSolWts, worstWts, numFeatures + 1);
```

```
    solutions[worst].error = randomSolError;
    continue;
}
```

Generating a candidate solution and computing its associated mean squared error is a relatively expensive operation because every training data item must be processed. So an alternative to consider is to attempt a random solution every so often, say, just once for every 100 iterations:

```
if (epoch % 100 == 0)
{
    // create and examine a random solution
}
```

Now at this point, no viable replacement for the worst solution was found, so the simplex shrinks in on itself by moving the worst and "other" solutions toward the best solution:

```
. . .
    for (int j = 0; j < numFeatures + 1; ++j)
      worstWts[j] = (worstWts[j] + bestWts[j]) / 2.0;
    solutions[worst].error = Error(trainData, solutions[worst].weights);

    for (int j = 0; j < numFeatures + 1; ++j)
      otherWts[j] = (otherWts[j] + bestWts[j]) / 2.0;
    solutions[other].error = Error(trainData, otherWts);

} // while
```

Here, the current worst and "other" solutions move halfway toward the best solution, as indicated by the 2.0 constants in the code. The definition of method Train concludes with:

```
. . .
    Array.Copy(solutions[best].weights, this.weights, this.numFeatures + 1);
    return this.weights;
}
```

The weights in the best Solution object are copied into class member array weights. A reference to the class member weights is returned so that the best weights can be used by other methods, such as ComputeDependent in particular, to make predictions on new, previously unseen data. An alternative to returning the best weights by reference is to make a new array, copy the values from the best solution into that array, and return by value.

Helper method CentroidWts computes the centroid used by simplex optimization. Recall the centroid is an average of the current best and "other" solutions:

```
private double[] CentroidWts(double[] otherWts, double[] bestWts)
{
    double[] result = new double[this.numFeatures + 1];
    for (int i = 0; i < result.Length; ++i)
      result[i] = (otherWts[i] + bestWts[i]) / 2.0;
    return result;
}
```

Helper method ExpandedWts is defined:

```
private double[] ExpandedWts(double[] centroidWts, double[] worstWts)
{
  double gamma = 2.0;
  double[] result = new double[this.numFeatures + 1];
  for (int i = 0; i < result.Length; ++i)
    result[i] = centroidWts[i] + (gamma * (centroidWts[i] - worstWts[i]));
  return result;
}
```

Here, local variable gamma controls how far the expanded candidate is from the centroid. Larger values of gamma tend to produce larger changes in the solutions in the beginning of processing at the expense of unneeded calculations later in the processing. Smaller values of gamma tend to produce smaller changes initially, but fewer calculations later.

Helper methods ReflectedWts and ContractedWts use the exact same pattern as method ExpandedWts:

```
private double[] ReflectedWts(double[] centroidWts, double[] worstWts)
{
  double alpha = 1.0;
  double[] result = new double[this.numFeatures + 1];
  for (int i = 0; i < result.Length; ++i)
    result[i] = centroidWts[i] + (alpha * (centroidWts[i] - worstWts[i]));
  return result;
}

private double[] ContractedWts(double[] centroidWts, double[] worstWts)
{
  double rho = -0.5;
  double[] result = new double[this.numFeatures + 1];
  for (int i = 0; i < result.Length; ++i)
    result[i] = centroidWts[i] + (rho * (centroidWts[i] - worstWts[i]));
  return result;
}
```

In method ReflectedWts, with an alpha value of 1.0, multiplying by alpha obviously has no effect, so in a production scenario you could just eliminate alpha altogether. There are several ways to improve the efficiency of these three helper methods, though at the minor expense of some loss of clarity. For example, notice that each method computes the quantity centroidWts[i] - worstWts[i]. This common value could be computed just once and then passed to each method along the lines of:

```
for (int i = 0; i < numFeatures + 1; ++i)
  delta[i] = centroidWts[i] - worstWts[i];

double[] expandedWts = ExpandedWts(delta);
. . .
double[] reflectedWts = ReflectedWts(delta);
// etc.
```

Helper method RandomSolutionWts is used to initialize the three current solutions (best, worst, other), and is also used, optionally, to probe when no replacement candidate (expanded, reflected, contracted) is better than the current worst solution. The method is defined:

```
private double[] RandomSolutionWts()
{
  double[] result = new double[this.numFeatures + 1];
  double lo = -10.0;
  double hi = 10.0;
  for (int i = 0; i < result.Length; ++i)
    result[i] = (hi - lo) * rnd.NextDouble() + lo;
  return result;
}
```

The method returns an array of weights where each value is a random number between -10.0 and +10.0, for example { 3.33, -0.17, 7.92, -5.05 }. Because it is assumed that all input x-values have been normalized, the majority of x-values will be between -10.0 and +10.0, so this range is also used for the weight values. Because these two values are hard-coded, in method RandomSolutionWts you could replace term (hi - lo) with the constant 20.0, and replace variable lo with -10.0. If your x-values are not normalized, it is quite possible that constraining weight values to the interval [-10.0, +10.0] could lead to a poor model when the magnitudes of different features vary greatly.

The Train method iterates a fixed number of times specified by the maxEpochs variable:

```
int epoch = 0;
while (epoch < maxEpochs)
{
  ++epoch;
  // search for best weights
}
```

An important, recurring theme in most machine learning training algorithms is that there are many ways to control when the main training loop terminates. For simplex optimization, there are two important options to consider. First, you may want to exit early if the Euclidean distance (difference) between the current best and worst solutions reaches some very low value indicating the simplex has collapsed on itself. Second, you may want to exit only when the mean squared error drops below some acceptable level, indicating your model is likely good enough.

Other Scenarios

This chapter explains binary logistic regression classification, where the dependent variable can take one of just two possible values. There are several techniques you can use to extend logistic regression to situations where the dependent variable can take one of three or more values, for example, predicting a person's political affiliation of Democrat, Republican, or Independent. The simplest approach is called one-versus-all. You would run logistic regression for Democrat versus "others", run a second time with Republican versus "others", and run a third time with Independent versus "others". That said, logistic regression classification is most often used for binary problems.

Logistic regression classification can handle problems where the predictor variables are numeric, such as the kidney score feature in the demo program, or categorical, such as the sex feature in the demo. For a categorical x-variable with two possible values, such as sex, the values are encoded as -1 or +1. For x-variables that have three or more possible values, the trick is to use a technique called 1-of-(N-1) encoding. For example, if three predictor values are "small","medium", and "large", the values would be encoded as (1, 0), (0, 1), and (-1, -1), respectively.

Chapter 3 Complete Demo Program Source Code

```
using System;
namespace LogisticRegression
{
  class LogisticProgram
  {
    static void Main(string[] args)
    {
      Console.WriteLine("\nBegin Logistic Regression Binary Classification demo");
      Console.WriteLine("Goal is to predict death (0 = false, 1 = true)");

      double[][] data = new double[30][];
      data[0] = new double[] { 48, +1, 4.40, 0 };
      data[1] = new double[] { 60, -1, 7.89, 1 };
      data[2] = new double[] { 51, -1, 3.48, 0 };
      data[3] = new double[] { 66, -1, 8.41, 1 };
      data[4] = new double[] { 40, +1, 3.05, 0 };
      data[5] = new double[] { 44, +1, 4.56, 0 };
      data[6] = new double[] { 80, -1, 6.91, 1 };
      data[7] = new double[] { 52, -1, 5.69, 0 };
      data[8] = new double[] { 56, -1, 4.01, 0 };
      data[9] = new double[] { 55, -1, 4.48, 0 };
      data[10] = new double[] { 72, +1, 5.97, 0 };
      data[11] = new double[] { 57, -1, 6.71, 1 };
      data[12] = new double[] { 50, -1, 6.40, 0 };
      data[13] = new double[] { 80, -1, 6.67, 1 };
      data[14] = new double[] { 69, +1, 5.79, 0 };
      data[15] = new double[] { 39, -1, 5.42, 0 };
      data[16] = new double[] { 68, -1, 7.61, 1 };
      data[17] = new double[] { 47, +1, 3.24, 0 };
      data[18] = new double[] { 45, +1, 4.29, 0 };
      data[19] = new double[] { 79, +1, 7.44, 1 };
      data[20] = new double[] { 44, -1, 2.55, 0 };
      data[21] = new double[] { 52, +1, 3.71, 0 };
      data[22] = new double[] { 80, +1, 7.56, 1 };
      data[23] = new double[] { 76, -1, 7.80, 1 };
      data[24] = new double[] { 51, -1, 5.94, 0 };
      data[25] = new double[] { 46, +1, 5.52, 0 };
      data[26] = new double[] { 48, -1, 3.25, 0 };
      data[27] = new double[] { 58, +1, 4.71, 0 };
      data[28] = new double[] { 44, +1, 2.52, 0 };
      data[29] = new double[] { 68, -1, 8.38, 1 };

      Console.WriteLine("\nRaw data: \n");
      Console.WriteLine("      Age      Sex      Kidney    Died");
      Console.WriteLine("===========================================");
      ShowData(data, 5, 2, true);

      Console.WriteLine("Normalizing age and kidney data");
      int[] columns = new int[] { 0, 2 };
      double[][] means = Normalize(data, columns); // normalize, save means and stdDevs
      Console.WriteLine("Done");

      Console.WriteLine("\nNormalized data: \n");
      ShowData(data, 5, 2, true);

      Console.WriteLine("Creating train (80%) and test (20%) matrices");
      double[][] trainData;
```

```
      double[][] testData;
      MakeTrainTest(data, 0, out trainData, out testData);
      Console.WriteLine("Done");

      Console.WriteLine("\nNormalized training data: \n");
      ShowData(trainData, 3, 2, true);

      //Console.WriteLine("\nFirst 3 rows and last row of normalized test data: \n");
      //ShowData(testData, 3, 2, true);

      int numFeatures = 3; // number of x-values (age, sex, kidney)
      Console.WriteLine("Creating LR binary classifier");
      LogisticClassifier lc = new LogisticClassifier(numFeatures);

      int maxEpochs = 100; // gives a representative demo
      Console.WriteLine("Setting maxEpochs = " + maxEpochs);
      Console.WriteLine("Starting training using simplex optimization");
      double[] bestWeights = lc.Train(trainData, maxEpochs, 33); // 33 = 'nice' demo
      Console.WriteLine("Training complete");

      Console.WriteLine("\nBest weights found:");
      ShowVector(bestWeights, 4, true);

      double trainAccuracy = lc.Accuracy(trainData, bestWeights);
      Console.WriteLine("Prediction accuracy on training data = " +
        trainAccuracy.ToString("F4"));

      double testAccuracy = lc.Accuracy(testData, bestWeights);
      Console.WriteLine("Prediction accuracy on test data = " +
        testAccuracy.ToString("F4"));

      //double[][] unknown = new double[1][];
      //unknown[0] = new double[] { 58.0, -1.0, 7.00 };
      //Normalize(unknown, columns, means);
      //int died = lc.ComputeDependent(unknown[0], bestWeights);
      //Console.WriteLine("Died = " + died);

      Console.WriteLine("\nEnd LR binary classification demo\n");
      Console.ReadLine();
    } // Main

    static double[][] Normalize(double[][] rawData, int[] columns)
    {
      // return means and sdtDevs of all columns for later use
      int numRows = rawData.Length;
      int numCols = rawData[0].Length;

      double[][] result = new double[2][]; // [0] = mean, [1] = stdDev
      for (int i = 0; i < 2; ++i)
        result[i] = new double[numCols];

      for (int c = 0; c < numCols; ++c)
      {
        // means of all cols
        double sum = 0.0;
        for (int r = 0; r < numRows; ++r)
          sum += rawData[r][c];
        double mean = sum / numRows;
        result[0][c] = mean; // save
```

```
    // stdDevs of all cols
    double sumSquares = 0.0;
    for (int r = 0; r < numRows; ++r)
      sumSquares += (rawData[r][c] - mean) * (rawData[r][c] - mean);
    double stdDev = Math.Sqrt(sumSquares / numRows);
    result[1][c] = stdDev;
  }

  // normalize
  for (int c = 0; c < columns.Length; ++c)
  {
    int j = columns[c]; // column to normalize
    double mean = result[0][j]; // mean of the col
    double stdDev = result[1][j];
    for (int i = 0; i < numRows; ++i)
      rawData[i][j] = (rawData[i][j] - mean) / stdDev;
  }
  return result;
}

static void Normalize(double[][] rawData, int[] columns, double[][] means)
{
  // normalize columns using supplied means and standard devs
  int numRows = rawData.Length;
  for (int c = 0; c < columns.Length; ++c) // each specified col
  {
    int j = columns[c]; // column to normalize
    double mean = means[0][j];
    double stdDev = means[1][j];
    for (int i = 0; i < numRows; ++i) // each row
      rawData[i][j] = (rawData[i][j] - mean) / stdDev;
  }
}

static void MakeTrainTest(double[][] allData, int seed,
  out double[][] trainData, out double[][] testData)
{
  Random rnd = new Random(seed);
  int totRows = allData.Length;
  int numTrainRows = (int)(totRows * 0.80); // 80% hard-coded
  int numTestRows = totRows - numTrainRows;
  trainData = new double[numTrainRows][];
  testData = new double[numTestRows][];

  double[][] copy = new double[allData.Length][]; // ref copy of all data
  for (int i = 0; i < copy.Length; ++i)
    copy[i] = allData[i];

  for (int i = 0; i < copy.Length; ++i) // scramble order
  {
    int r = rnd.Next(i, copy.Length); // use Fisher-Yates
    double[] tmp = copy[r];
    copy[r] = copy[i];
    copy[i] = tmp;
  }
  for (int i = 0; i < numTrainRows; ++i)
    trainData[i] = copy[i];

  for (int i = 0; i < numTestRows; ++i)
```

```
      testData[i] = copy[i + numTrainRows];
  } // MakeTrainTest


  static void ShowData(double[][] data, int numRows,
    int decimals, bool indices)
  {
    for (int i = 0; i < numRows; ++i)
    {
      if (indices == true)
        Console.Write("[" + i.ToString().PadLeft(2) + "] ");
      for (int j = 0; j < data[i].Length; ++j)
      {
        double v = data[i][j];
        if (v >= 0.0)
          Console.Write(" "); // '+'
        Console.Write(v.ToString("F" + decimals) + "   ");
      }
      Console.WriteLine("");
    }
    Console.WriteLine(". . .");
    int lastRow = data.Length - 1;
    if (indices == true)
      Console.Write("[" + lastRow.ToString().PadLeft(2) + "] ");
    for (int j = 0; j < data[lastRow].Length; ++j)
    {
      double v = data[lastRow][j];
      if (v >= 0.0)
        Console.Write(" "); // '+'
      Console.Write(v.ToString("F" + decimals) + "   ");
    }
    Console.WriteLine("\n");
  }

  static void ShowVector(double[] vector, int decimals, bool newLine)
  {
    for (int i = 0; i < vector.Length; ++i)
      Console.Write(vector[i].ToString("F" + decimals) + " ");
    Console.WriteLine("");
    if (newLine == true)
      Console.WriteLine("");
  }
} // Program

public class LogisticClassifier
{
  private int numFeatures; // number of independent variables aka features
  private double[] weights; // b0 = constant
  private Random rnd;

  public LogisticClassifier(int numFeatures)
  {
    this.numFeatures = numFeatures; // number of features/predictors
    this.weights = new double[numFeatures + 1]; // [0] = b0 constant
  }

  public double[] Train(double[][] trainData, int maxEpochs, int seed)
  {
    // sort 3 solutions (small error to large)
```

```
// compute centroid
// if expanded is better than worst replace
// else if reflected is better than worst, replace
// else if contracted is better than worst, replace
// else if random is better than worst, replace
// else shrink

this.rnd = new Random(seed); // so we can implement restart if wanted

Solution[] solutions = new Solution[3]; // best, worst, other

// initialize to random values
for (int i = 0; i < 3; ++i)
{
  solutions[i] = new Solution(numFeatures);
  solutions[i].weights = RandomSolutionWts();
  solutions[i].error = Error(trainData, solutions[i].weights);
}

int best = 0;  // for solutions[idx].error
int other = 1;
int worst = 2;

int epoch = 0;
while (epoch < maxEpochs)
{
  ++epoch;
  Array.Sort(solutions); // [0] = best, [1] = other, [2] = worst
  double[] bestWts = solutions[0].weights; // convenience only
  double[] otherWts = solutions[1].weights;
  double[] worstWts = solutions[2].weights;

  double[] centroidWts = CentroidWts(otherWts, bestWts); // an average

  double[] expandedWts = ExpandedWts(centroidWts, worstWts);
  double expandedError = Error(trainData, expandedWts);
  if (expandedError < solutions[worst].error) // expanded better than worst?
  {
    Array.Copy(expandedWts, worstWts, numFeatures + 1); // replace worst
    solutions[worst].error = expandedError;
    continue;
  }

  double[] reflectedWts = ReflectedWts(centroidWts, worstWts);
  double reflectedError = Error(trainData, reflectedWts);
  if (reflectedError < solutions[worst].error) // relected better than worst?
  {
    Array.Copy(reflectedWts, worstWts, numFeatures + 1);
    solutions[worst].error = reflectedError;
    continue;
  }

  double[] contractedWts = ContractedWts(centroidWts, worstWts);
  double contractedError = Error(trainData, contractedWts);
  if (contractedError < solutions[worst].error) // contracted better than worst?
  {
    Array.Copy(contractedWts, worstWts, numFeatures + 1);
    solutions[worst].error = contractedError;
    continue;
  }
```

```
      double[] randomSolWts = RandomSolutionWts();
      double randomSolError = Error(trainData, randomSolWts);
      if (randomSolError < solutions[worst].error)
      {
        Array.Copy(randomSolWts, worstWts, numFeatures + 1);
        solutions[worst].error = randomSolError;
        continue;
      }

      // couldn't find a replacement for worst so shrink
      // worst -> towards best
      for (int j = 0; j < numFeatures + 1; ++j)
        worstWts[j] = (worstWts[j] + bestWts[j]) / 2.0;
      solutions[worst].error = Error(trainData, worstWts);

      // 'other' -> towards best
      for (int j = 0; j < numFeatures + 1; ++j)
        otherWts[j] = (otherWts[j] + bestWts[j]) / 2.0;
      solutions[other].error = Error(trainData, otherWts);

    } // while

    // copy best weights found, return by reference
    Array.Copy(solutions[best].weights, this.weights, this.numFeatures + 1);
    return this.weights;
}

private double[] CentroidWts(double[] otherWts, double[] bestWts)
{
  double[] result = new double[this.numFeatures + 1];
  for (int i = 0; i < result.Length; ++i)
    result[i] = (otherWts[i] + bestWts[i]) / 2.0;
  return result;
}

private double[] ExpandedWts(double[] centroidWts, double[] worstWts)
{
  double gamma = 2.0; // how far from centroid
  double[] result = new double[this.numFeatures + 1];
  for (int i = 0; i < result.Length; ++i)
    result[i] = centroidWts[i] + (gamma * (centroidWts[i] - worstWts[i]));
  return result;
}

private double[] ReflectedWts(double[] centroidWts, double[] worstWts)
{
  double alpha = 1.0; // how far from centroid
  double[] result = new double[this.numFeatures + 1];
  for (int i = 0; i < result.Length; ++i)
    result[i] = centroidWts[i] + (alpha * (centroidWts[i] - worstWts[i]));
  return result;
}

private double[] ContractedWts(double[] centroidWts, double[] worstWts)
{
  double rho = -0.5;
  double[] result = new double[this.numFeatures + 1];
  for (int i = 0; i < result.Length; ++i)
```

```
      result[i] = centroidWts[i] + (rho * (centroidWts[i] - worstWts[i]));
    return result;
}

private double[] RandomSolutionWts()
{
    double[] result = new double[this.numFeatures + 1];
    double lo = -10.0;
    double hi = 10.0;
    for (int i = 0; i < result.Length; ++i)
      result[i] = (hi - lo) * rnd.NextDouble() + lo;
    return result;
}

private double Error(double[][] trainData, double[] weights)
{
    // mean squared error using supplied weights
    int yIndex = trainData[0].Length - 1; // y-value (0/1) is last column
    double sumSquaredError = 0.0;
    for (int i = 0; i < trainData.Length; ++i) // each data
    {
      double computed = ComputeOutput(trainData[i], weights);
      double desired = trainData[i][yIndex]; // ex: 0.0 or 1.0
      sumSquaredError += (computed - desired) * (computed - desired);
    }
    return sumSquaredError / trainData.Length;
}

public double ComputeOutput(double[] dataItem, double[] weights)
{
    double z = 0.0;

    z += weights[0]; // the b0 constant
    for (int i = 0; i < weights.Length - 1; ++i) // data might include Y
      z += (weights[i + 1] * dataItem[i]); // skip first weight
    return 1.0 / (1.0 + Math.Exp(-z));
}

public int ComputeDependent(double[] dataItem, double[] weights)
{
    double sum = ComputeOutput(dataItem, weights);

    if (sum <= 0.5)
      return 0;
    else
      return 1;
}

public double Accuracy(double[][] trainData, double[] weights)
{
    int numCorrect = 0;
    int numWrong = 0;
    int yIndex = trainData[0].Length - 1;
    for (int i = 0; i < trainData.Length; ++i)
    {
      double computed = ComputeDependent(trainData[i], weights); // implicit cast
      double desired = trainData[i][yIndex]; // 0.0 or 1.0

      if (computed == desired) // risky?
        ++numCorrect;
```

```
      else
        ++numWrong;

      //double closeness = 0.00000001;
      //if (Math.Abs(computed - desired) < closeness)
      //   ++numCorrect;
      //else
      //   ++numWrong;
    }
    return (numCorrect * 1.0) / (numWrong + numCorrect);
  }

  private class Solution : IComparable<Solution>
  {
    public double[] weights; // a potential solution
    public double error;     // MSE of weights

    public Solution(int numFeatures)
    {
      this.weights = new double[numFeatures + 1]; // problem dim + constant
      this.error = 0.0;
    }

    public int CompareTo(Solution other) // low-to-high error
    {
      if (this.error < other.error)
        return -1;
      else if (this.error > other.error)
        return 1;
      else
        return 0;
    }
  } // Solution

} // LogisticClassifier
} // ns
```

Chapter 4 Naive Bayes Classification

Introduction

Most machine learning classification techniques work strictly with numeric data. For these techniques, any non-numeric predictor values, such as male and female, must be converted to numeric values, such as -1 and +1. Naive Bayes is a classification technique that is an exception. It classifies and makes predictions with categorical data.

The "naive" (which means unsophisticated in ordinary usage) in naive Bayes means that all the predictor features are assumed to be independent. For example, suppose you want to predict a person's political inclination, conservative or liberal, based on the person's job (such as cook, doctor, etc.), sex (male or female), and income (low, medium, or high). Naive Bayes assumes job, sex, and income are all independent. This is obviously not true in many situations. In this example, job and income are almost certainly related. In spite of the crude independence assumption, naive Bayes classification is often very effective when working with categorical data.

The "Bayes" refers to Bayes' theorem. Bayes' theorem is a fairly simple equation characterized by a "given" condition to find values such as "the probability that a person is a doctor, *given* that they are a political conservative." The ideas behind Bayes' theorem are very deep, conceptually and philosophically, but fortunately, applying the theorem when performing naive Bayes classification is relatively simple in principle (although the implementation details are a bit tricky).

A good way to understand naive Bayes classification, and to see where this chapter is headed, is to examine the screenshot of a demo program, shown in **Figure 4-a**. The goal of the demo program is to predict the political inclination (conservative or liberal) of a person based on his or her job (analyst, barista, cook, or doctor), sex (male, female), and annual income (low, medium, high). Notice each feature is categorical, not numeric.

The demo program starts with 30 (artificially constructed) data items. The first two items are:

```
analyst   male     high    conservative
barista   female   low     liberal
```

The independent X predictor variables, job, sex, and income, are in the first three columns, and the dependent Y variable to predict, politics, is in the last column.

The demo splits the 30-item data set into an 80% (24 data items) training data set and a 20% (6 data items) test data set in such a way that the data items are randomly assigned to one of the two sets. The training data set is used to construct the naive Bayes predictive model, and the test data set is used to give an estimate of the model's accuracy when presented with new, previously unseen data.

Next, the demo uses the training data and naive Bayes mathematics to construct a predictive model. Behind the scenes, each feature-column is assumed to be independent.

After creating the model, the demo computes the model's accuracy on the training data set and on the test data set. The model correctly predicts 91.67% of the training items (22 out of 24) and 83.33% of the test items (5 out of 6).

```
file:///F:/Data/MachineLearningSuccinctly/Code/Chapter4/NaiveBayes/bin/Debug/NaiveB...  _ |□| x|

Begin Naive Bayes classification demo
Goal is to predict (liberal/conservative) from job, sex and income

The raw data is:

[  0]         analyst           male            high      conservative
[  1]         barista           female          low        liberal
[  2]         cook              male            medium    conservative
[  3]         doctor            female          medium    conservative
[  4]         analyst           female          low        liberal

[29]          barista           male            medium    conservative

Splitting data into 80%-20% train and test sets
Done

Training data:

[  0]         doctor            male            medium    conservative
[  1]         cook              female          low        liberal
[  2]         cook              female          low        liberal
[  3]         analyst           male            high      conservative
[  4]         barista           male            medium    conservative

[23]          barista           female          medium     liberal

Test data:

[  0]         cook              female          high       liberal
[  1]         doctor            female          medium    conservative
[  2]         barista           female          low        liberal
[  3]         doctor            female          high      conservative
[  4]         analyst           male            medium    conservative
[  5]         analyst           male            low        liberal

Creating Naive Bayes classifier object
Training classifier using training data
Done

Accuracy of model on train data = 0.9167
Accuracy of model on test data  = 0.8333

Predicting politics for job = barista, sex = female, income = medium

Probability of liberal      = 0.6550
Probability of conservative = 0.3450

End Naive Bayes classification demo
```

Figure 4-a: Naive Bayes Classification Demo Program

Next, the demo program uses the model to predict the political inclination of a hypothetical person who has a job as a barista, is a female, and has a medium income. According to the model, the probability that the hypothetical person has a liberal inclination is 0.6550 and the probability that the person is a conservative is 0.3450; therefore, the unknown person is predicted to be a liberal.

The sections that follow will describe how naive Bayes classification works, and present and explain in detail the code for the demo program. Although there are existing systems and API sets that can perform naive Bayes classification, being able to write your own prediction system gives you total control of the many possible implementation options, avoids unforeseen legal issues, and can give you a good understanding of how other systems work so you can use them more effectively.

Understanding Naive Bayes

Suppose, as in the demo program, you want to predict the political inclination (conservative or liberal) of a person whose job is barista, sex is female, and income is medium. You would compute the probability that the person is a conservative, and the probability that the person is a liberal, and then predict the outcome with the higher probability.

Expressed mathematically, the problem is to find these two values:

P(conservative) = P(conservative | barista & female & medium)

P(liberal) = P(liberal | barista & female & medium)

The top equation is sometimes read as, "the probability that Y is conservative, given that X is barista and female and medium." Similarly, the bottom equation is, "the probability that Y is liberal, given that X is barista and female and medium."

To compute these probabilities, quantities that are sometimes called partials are needed. The partial (denoted PP) for the first dependent variable is:

PP(conservative) =
P(barista | conservative) * P(female | conservative) * P(medium | conservative) *
P(conservative)

Similarly, the partial for the second dependent variable is:

PP(liberal) =
P(barista | liberal) * P(female | liberal) * P(medium | liberal) * P(liberal)

If these two partials can somehow be computed, then the two probabilities needed to make a prediction are:

P(conservative) = PP(conservative) / (PP(conservative) + PP(liberal))

P(liberal) = PP(liberal) / (PP(conservative) + PP(liberal))

Notice the denominator is the same in each case. This term is sometimes called the *evidence*. The challenge is to find the two partials. In this example, each partial has four terms multiplied together. Consider the first term in PP(conservative), which is P(barista | conservative), read as "the probability of a barista given that the person is a conservative." Bayes' theorem gives:

P(barista | conservative) = Count(barista & conservative) / Count(conservative)

Here, Count is just a simple count of the number of applicable data items. In essence, this equation looks only at those people who are conservative, and finds what percentage of them are baristas. The quantity Count(barista & conservative) is called a joint count.

The next two terms for the partial for conservative, P(female | conservative) and PP(medium | conservative), can be found in the same way:

P(female | conservative) = Count(female & conservative) / Count(conservative)
P(medium | conservative) = Count(medium & conservative) / Count(conservative)

The last term for the partial of conservative is P(conservative), in words, "the probability that a person is a conservative." This can be found easily:

P(conservative) = Count(conservative) / (Count(conservative) + Count(liberal))

In other words, the probability that a person is a conservative is just the number of people who are conservatives, divided by the total number of people.

Putting this all together, if the problem is to find the probability that a person is a conservative and also the probability that the person is a liberal, if the person is a female barista with medium income, you need the partial for conservative and the partial for liberal. The partial for conservative is:

PP(conservative) =

P(barista | conservative) * P(female | conservative) * P(medium | conservative) * P(conservative) =

Count(barista & conservative) / Count(conservative) *
Count(female & conservative) / Count(conservative) *
Count(medium & conservative) / Count(conservative) *
Count(conservative) / (Count(conservative) + Count(liberal))

And the partial for liberal is:

PP(liberal) =

P(barista | liberal) * P(female | liberal) * P(medium | liberal) * P(liberal) =

Count(barista & liberal) / Count(liberal) *
Count(female & liberal) / Count(liberal) *
Count(medium & liberal) / Count(liberal) *
Count(liberal) / (Count(conservative) + Count(liberal))

And the two probabilities are:

P(conservative) = PP(conservative) / (PP(conservative) + PP(liberal))

P(liberal) = PP(liberal) / (PP(conservative) + PP(liberal))

Each piece of the puzzle is just a simple count, but there are many pieces. If you review the calculations carefully, you'll note that to compute any possible probability, for example P(liberal | cook & male & low) or P(conservative | analyst & female & high), you need the joint counts of every feature value with every dependent value, like "doctor & conservative", "male & liberal", "low & conservative", and so on. You also need the count of each dependent value.

To predict the political inclination of a female barista with medium income, the demo program computes P(conservative | barista & female & medium) and P(liberal | barista & female & medium) as follows.

First, the program scans the 24-item training data and finds all the relevant joint counts, and adds 1 to each count. The results are:

Count(barista & conservative)   = 3 + 1   = 4
Count(female & conservative)   = 3 + 1   = 4
Count(medium & conservative)   = 11 + 1 = 12
Count(barista & liberal)   = 2 + 1   = 3
Count(female & liberal)   = 8 + 1   = 9
Count(medium & liberal)   = 5 + 1   = 6

If you refer back to how partials are computed, you'll see they consist of several joint count terms multiplied together. If any joint count is 0, the entire product will be 0, and the calculation falls apart. Adding 1 to each joint count prevents this, and is called Laplacian smoothing.

Next, the program scans the 24-item training data and calculates the counts of the dependent variables and adds 3 (the number of features) to each:

Count(conservative) = 15 + 3 = 18
Count(liberal) = 9 + 3 = 12

Adding the number of features, 3 in this case, to each dependent variable count balances the 1 added to each of the three joint counts. Now the partials are computed like so:

PP(conservative) =

Count(barista & conservative) / Count(conservative) *
Count(female & conservative) / Count(conservative) *
Count(medium & conservative) / Count(conservative) *
Count(conservative) / (Count(conservative) + Count(liberal)) =

= (4 / 18) * (4 / 18) * (12 / 18) * (18 / 30)

= 0.2222 * 0.2222 * 0.6667 * 0.6000

= 0.01975 (rounded).

PP(liberal) =

Count(barista & liberal) / Count(liberal) *
Count(female & liberal) / Count(liberal) *
Count(medium & liberal) / Count(liberal) *
Count(liberal) / (Count(conservative) + Count(liberal)) =

= (3 / 12) * (9 / 12) * (6 / 12) * (12 / 30)

= 0.2500 * 0.7500 * 0.5000 * 0.4000

= 0.03750.

Using the partials, the final probabilities are computed:

P(conservative) = PP(conservative) / (PP(conservative) + PP(liberal))
                = 0.01975 / (0.01975 + 0.03750)
                = 0.3450 (rounded)

P(liberal) = PP(liberal) / (PP(conservative) + PP(liberal))
           = 0.03750 / (0.01975 + 0.03750)
           = 0.6550 (rounded)

If you refer to the screenshot in **Figure 4-a**, you'll see these two probability values displayed. Because the probability of liberal is greater than the probability of conservative, the prediction is that a female barista with medium income will most likely be a political liberal.

Demo Program Structure

The overall structure of the demo program, with a few minor edits to save space, is presented in **Listing 4-a**. To create the demo program, I launched Visual Studio and created a new C# console application project named NaiveBayes.

After the template code loaded into the editor, I removed all using statements at the top of the source code, except for the reference to the top-level System namespace, and the one to the Collections.Generic namespace. In the Solution Explorer window, I renamed file Program.cs to the more descriptive BayesProgram.cs, and Visual Studio automatically renamed class Program to BayesProgram.

```
using System;
using System.Collections.Generic;
namespace NaiveBayes
{
  class BayesProgram
  {
    static void Main(string[] args)
    {
      Console.WriteLine("Begin Naive Bayes classification demo");
      Console.WriteLine("Goal is to predict (liberal/conservative) from job, " +
        "sex and income");

      string[][] rawData = new string[30][];
      rawData[0] = new string[] { "analyst", "male", "high", "conservative" };
      // etc.
      rawData[29] = new string[] { "barista", "male", "medium", "conservative" };

      Console.WriteLine("The raw data is: ");
      ShowData(rawData, 5, true);

      Console.WriteLine("Splitting data into 80%-20% train and test sets");
      string[][] trainData;
      string[][] testData;
```

```
MakeTrainTest(rawData, 15, out trainData, out testData); // seed = 15
Console.WriteLine("Done");

Console.WriteLine("Training data: ");
ShowData(trainData, 5, true);

Console.WriteLine("Test data: ");
ShowData(testData, 5, true);

Console.WriteLine("Creating Naive Bayes classifier object");
BayesClassifier bc = new BayesClassifier();
bc.Train(trainData);
Console.WriteLine("Done");

double trainAccuracy = bc.Accuracy(trainData);
Console.WriteLine("Accuracy of model on train data = " +
  trainAccuracy.ToString("F4"));
double testAccuracy = bc.Accuracy(testData);
Console.WriteLine("Accuracy of model on test data  = " +
  testAccuracy.ToString("F4"));

Console.WriteLine("Predicting politics for job = barista, sex = female, " +
  "income = medium ");
string[] features = new string[] { "barista", "female", "medium" };

string liberal = "liberal";
double pLiberal = bc.Probability(liberal, features);
Console.WriteLine("Probability of liberal  = " +
  pLiberal.ToString("F4"));

string conservative = "conservative";
double pConservative = bc.Probability(conservative, features);
Console.WriteLine("Probability of conservative = " +
  pConservative.ToString("F4"));

Console.WriteLine("End Naive Bayes classification demo ");
Console.ReadLine();
} // Main

static void MakeTrainTest(string[][] allData, int seed,
  out string[][] trainData, out string[][] testData) { . . }

static void ShowData(string[][] rawData, int numRows, bool indices) { . . }
} // Program

public class BayesClassifier { . . }
} // ns
```

Listing 4-a: Naive Bayes Demo Program Structure

The demo program class has two static helper methods. Method MakeTrainTest randomly splits the source data into an 80% training set and 20% test data. The 80-20 split is hard-coded, and you might want to parameterize the percentage of training data. Helper method ShowData displays an array-of-arrays style matrix of string values to the shell.

All the Bayes classification logic is contained in a single program-defined class named BayesClassifier. All the program logic is contained in the Main method. The Main method begins by setting up 30 hard-coded (job, sex, income, politics) data items in an array-of-arrays style matrix:

```
static void Main(string[] args)
{
  Console.WriteLine("\nBegin Naive Bayes classification demo");
  Console.WriteLine("Goal is to predict (liberal/conservative) from job, " +
    "sex and income\n");
  string[][] rawData = new string[30][];
  rawData[0] = new string[] { "analyst", "male", "high", "conservative" };
  rawData[1] = new string[] { "barista", "female", "low", "liberal" };
  // etc.
  rawData[29] = new string[] { "barista", "male", "medium", "conservative" };
  . . .
```

In most realistic scenarios, your source data would be stored in a text file, and you would load it into a matrix in memory using a helper method named something like LoadData. Here, the dependent variable, politics, is assumed to be in the last column of the data matrix.

Next, the demo displays a part of the source data, and then creates the training and test sets:

```
Console.WriteLine("The raw data is: \n");
ShowData(rawData, 5, true);

Console.WriteLine("Splitting data into 80%-20% train and test sets");
string[][] trainData;
string[][] testData;
MakeTrainTest(rawData, 15, out trainData, out testData);
Console.WriteLine("Done \n");
```

The 5 argument passed to method ShowData is the number of rows to display, not including the last line of data, which is always displayed by default. The 15 argument passed to method MakeTrainTest is used as a seed value for a Random object, which randomizes how data items are assigned to either the training or test sets.

Next, the demo displays the first five, and last line, of the training and test sets:

```
Console.WriteLine("Training data: \n");
ShowData(trainData, 5, true);

Console.WriteLine("Test data: \n");
ShowData(testData, 5, true);
```

The true argument passed to ShowData directs the method to display row indices. In order to see the entire training data set so you can see how Bayes joint counts were calculated in the previous section, you could pass 23 as the number of rows.

Next, the classifier is created and trained:

```
Console.WriteLine("Creating Naive Bayes classifier object");
Console.WriteLine("Training classifier using training data");
```

```
BayesClassifier bc = new BayesClassifier();
bc.Train(trainData);
Console.WriteLine("Done \n");
```

Most of the work is done by method Train. In the case of naive Bayes, the Train method scans through the training data and calculates all the joint counts between feature values (like "doctor" and "high") and dependent values ("conservative" or "liberal"). The Train method also calculates the count of each dependent variable value.

After the model finishes the training process, the accuracy of the model on the training and test sets are calculated and displayed like so:

```
double trainAccuracy = bc.Accuracy(trainData);
Console.WriteLine("Accuracy of model on train data = " +
trainAccuracy.ToString("F4"));
double testAccuracy = bc.Accuracy(testData);
Console.WriteLine("Accuracy of model on test data  = " +
testAccuracy.ToString("F4"));
```

Next, the demo indirectly makes a prediction by computing the probability that a female barista with medium income is a liberal:

```
Console.WriteLine("\nPredicting politics for job = barista, sex = female, "
        + "income = medium \n");
string[] features = new string[] { "barista", "female", "medium" };

string liberal = "liberal";
double pLiberal = bc.Probability(liberal, features);
Console.WriteLine("Probability of liberal   = " + pLiberal.ToString("F4"));
```

Note that because this is a binary classification problem, only one probability is needed to make a classification decision. If the probability of either liberal or conservative is greater than 0.5, then because the sum of the probabilities of liberal and conservative is 1.0, the probability of the other political inclination must be less than 0.5, and vice versa.

The demo concludes by computing the probability that a female barista with medium income is a conservative:

```
. . .
  string conservative = "conservative";
  double pConservative = bc.Probability(conservative, features);
  Console.WriteLine("Probability of conservative = " + pConservative.ToString("F4"));

  Console.WriteLine("\nEnd Naive Bayes classification demo\n");
  Console.ReadLine();
} // Main
```

An option to consider is to write a class method Predicted, which returns the dependent variable with higher probability.

Defining the BayesClassifer Class

The structure of the program-defined class BayesClassifier is presented in **Listing 4-b**. The class has three data members and exposes four public methods. The key to understanding the implementation so that you can modify it if necessary to meet your own needs, is to understand the three data structures. The class data structures are illustrated in **Figure 4-b**.

```
public class BayesClassifier
{
    private Dictionary<string, int>[] stringToInt;
    private int[][][] jointCounts;
    private int[] dependentCounts;

    public BayesClassifier() { . . }
    public void Train(string[][] trainData) { . . }
    public double Probability(string yValue, string[] xValues) { . . }
    public double Accuracy(string[][] data) { . . }
}
```

Listing 4-b: The BayesClassifier Class Structure

Data member stringToInt is an array of Dictionary objects. There is one Dictionary object for each column of data, and each Dictionary maps a string value, such as "barista" or "conservative", to a zero-based integer. For example, stringToInt[0]["doctor"] returns the integer value for feature 0 (job), value "doctor". The zero-based integer is used as an index into the other data structures.

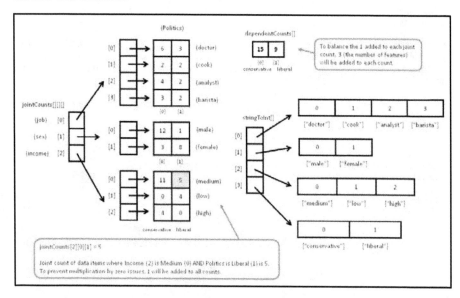

Figure 4-b: Naive Bayes Key Data Structures

The integer index value for a string feature value is the order in which the feature value is encountered when the training method scans the training data. For example, for the demo program, the first five lines of the training data generated by method MakeTrainTest are:

```
[0]   doctor      male    medium    conservative
[1]     cook    female       low         liberal
[2]     cook    female       low         liberal
[3]  analyst      male      high    conservative
[4]  barista      male    medium    conservative
```

When method Train scans the first column of the training data, it will assign "doctor" = 0, "cook" = 1, "analyst" = 2, and "barista" = 3. Similarly, after scanning, the values "male" = 0, "female" = 1, "medium" = 0, "low" = 1, "high" = 2, "conservative" = 0, and "liberal" = 1 will be stored into the stringToInt Dictionary objects. Note that these assignments are likely to change if method MakeTrainTest uses a different seed value and generates a different set of training data.

Class data member jointCounts holds the joint count of each possible pair of feature value and dependent value. For the demo example, there are a total of nine feature values: analyst, barista, cook, doctor, male, female, low, medium, and high. There are two dependent values: conservative and liberal. Therefore there are a total of 9 * 2 = 18 joint counts for the example: (analyst & conservative), (analyst & liberal), (barista & conservative) . . . , (high & liberal).

The expression jointCounts[2][0][1] holds the count of training items where feature 2 (income) equals value 0 (medium), and dependent 1 (liberal). Recall that each joint count has 1 added to avoid multiplication by zero (Laplacian smoothing).

Class member dependentCounts holds the number of each dependent variable. For example, the expression dependentCounts[0] holds the number of training items where the dependent value is 0 (conservative). Recall that each cell in array dependentCounts has 3 (the number of features for the problem) added to balance the 1 added to each joint count.

The class constructor is short and simple:

```
public BayesClassifier()
{
  this.stringToInt = null;
  this.jointCounts = null;
  this.dependentCounts = null;
}
```

In many OOP implementation scenarios, a class constructor allocates memory for the key member arrays and matrices. However, for naive Bayes, the number of cells to allocate in each of the three data structures will not be known until the training data is presented, so method Train will perform allocation.

One design alternative to consider is to pass the training data to the constructor. This design has some very subtle issues, both favorable and unfavorable, compared to having the training method perform allocation. A second design alternative is to pass the constructor integer parameters that hold the number of features, the number of distinct values in each feature, and the number of distinct dependent variable values.

The Training Method

Many machine classification algorithms work by creating some mathematical function that accepts feature values that are numeric and returns a numeric value that represents the predicted class. Examples of math-equation based algorithms include logistic regression classification, neural network classification, perceptron classification, support vector machine classification, and others. In these algorithms, the training process typically involves finding the values for a set of numeric constants, usually called the weights, which are used by the predicting equation.

Naive Bayes classification training does not search for a set of weights. Instead, the training simply scans the training data and calculates joint feature-dependent counts, and the counts of the dependent variable. These counts are used by the naive Bayes equations to compute the probability of a dependent class, given a set of feature values. In this sense, naive Bayes training is relatively simple.

The definition of method Train begins with:

```
public void Train(string[][] trainData)
{
  int numRows = trainData.Length;
  int numCols = trainData[0].Length;
  this.stringToInt = new Dictionary<string, int>[numCols];
. . .
```

Method Train works directly with an array-of-arrays style matrix of string values. An alternative is to preprocess the training data, and convert each categorical value, such as "doctor", into its corresponding integer value (0) and store this data in an integer matrix.

The array of Dictionary objects is allocated with the number of columns, and so includes the dependent variable, political inclination, in the demo. An important assumption is that the dependent variable is located in the last column of the training matrix.

Next, the dictionaries for each feature are instantiated and populated:

```
for (int col = 0; col < numCols; ++col)
{
  stringToInt[col] = new Dictionary<string, int>();

  int idx = 0;
  for (int row = 0; row < numRows; ++row)
  {
    string s = trainData[row][col];
    if (stringToInt[col].ContainsKey(s) == false) // first time seen
    {
      stringToInt[col].Add(s, idx); // ex: doctor -> 0
      ++idx; // prepare for next string
    }
  } // each row
} // each col
```

The training matrix is processed column by column. As each new feature value is discovered in a column, its index, in variable idx, is saved. The .NET generic Dictionary collection is fairly sophisticated. The purpose of storing each value's index is so that the index can be looked up quickly. An alternative is to store each distinct column value in a string array. Then the cell index is the value's index. But this approach would require a linear search through the string array.

Next, the jointCounts data structure is allocated like this:

```
this.jointCounts = new int[numCols - 1][][]; // number features

for (int c = 0; c < numCols - 1; ++c) // not y-column
{
  int count = this.stringToInt[c].Count;
  jointCounts[c] = new int[count][];
}

for (int i = 0; i < jointCounts.Length; ++i)
  for (int j = 0; j < jointCounts[i].Length; ++j)
    jointCounts[i][j] = new int[2]; // binary classification
```

For me at least, when working with data structures such as jointCounts, it's absolutely necessary to sketch a diagram, similar to the one in **Figure 4-b**, to avoid making mistakes. Working from left to right, the first dimension of jointCounts is allocated with the number of features (three in the demo). Then each of those references is allocated with the number of distinct values for that feature. For example, feature 0, job, has four distinct values. The number of distinct values is stored as the Count property of the string-to-int Dictionary collection for the feature.

The last dimension of jointCounts is allocated with hard-coded size 2. This makes the class strictly a binary classifier. To extend the implementation to a multiclass classifier, you'd just replace the 2 with the number of distinct dependent variable values:

```
int numDependent = stringToInt[stringToInt.Length - 1].Count;
jointCounts[i][j] = new int[numDependent];
```

Next, each cell in jointCounts is initialized with 1 to avoid any cell being 0, which would cause trouble:

```
for (int i = 0; i < jointCounts.Length; ++i)
  for (int j = 0; j < jointCounts[i].Length; ++j)
    for (int k = 0; k < jointCounts[i][j].Length; ++k)
      jointCounts[i][j][k] = 1;
```

Working with a data structure that has three index dimensions is not trivial, and can take some time to figure out. Next, method Train walks through each training data item and increments the appropriate cell in the jointCounts data structure:

```
for (int i = 0; i < numRows; ++i)
{
  string yString = trainData[i][numCols - 1]; // dependent value
  int depIndex = stringToInt[numCols - 1][yString]; // corresponding index
  for (int j = 0; j < numCols - 1; ++j)
  {
```

```
    int attIndex = j; // aka feature, index
    string xString = trainData[i][j]; // like "male"
    int valIndex = stringToInt[j][xString]; // corresponding index
    ++jointCounts[attIndex][valIndex][depIndex];
  }
}
```

Next, method Train allocates the data structure that stores the number of data items with each of the possible dependent values, and initializes the count in each cell to the number of features to use Laplacian smoothing:

```
this.dependentCounts = new int[2]; // binary
for (int i = 0; i < dependentCounts.Length; ++i) // Laplacian
  dependentCounts[i] = numCols - 1; // number features
```

The hard-coded 2 makes this strictly a binary classifier, so you may want to modify the code to handle multiclass problems. As before, you can use the Count property of the Dictionary object for the column to determine the number of distinct dependent variable values. Here, the number of features is the number of columns of the training data matrix, less 1, to account for the dependent variable in the last column.

Method Train concludes by walking through the training data matrix, and counts and stores the number of each dependent variable value, conservative and liberal, in the demo:

```
. . .
  for (int i = 0; i < trainData.Length; ++i)
  {
    string yString = trainData[i][numCols - 1]; // 'conservative' or 'liberal'
    int yIndex = stringToInt[numCols - 1][yString]; // 0 or 1
    ++dependentCounts[yIndex];
  }
  return;
}
```

Here, I use an explicit return keyword for no reason other than to note that it is possible. In a production environment, it's fairly important to follow a standard set of style guidelines that presumably addresses things like using an explicit return with a void method.

Method Probability

Class method Probability returns the Bayesian probability of a specified dependent class value given a set of feature values. In essence, method Probability is the prediction method. For example, for the demo data, to compute the probability that a person has a political inclination of liberal, given that they have a job of doctor, sex of male, and income of high, you could call:

```
string[] featureVals = new string[] { "doctor", "male", "high" };
double pLib = bc.Probability("liberal", featureVals); // prob person is liberal
```

For binary classification, if this probability is greater than 0.5, you would conclude the person has a liberal political inclination. If the probability is less than 0.5, you'd conclude the person is a conservative.

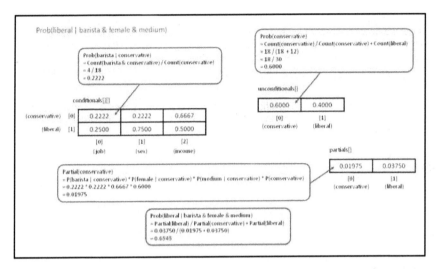

Figure 4-c: Computing a Bayesian Probability

The Probability method uses a matrix, conditionals, and two arrays, unconditionals and partials, to store the values needed to compute the partials for each dependent variable value, and then uses the two partials to compute the requested probability. Those data structures are illustrated in **Figure 4-c**.

The method's definition begins:

```
public double Probability(string yValue, string[] xValues)
{
  int numFeatures = xValues.Length;
  double[][] conditionals = new double[2][]; // binary
  for (int i = 0; i < 2; ++i)
    conditionals[i] = new double[numFeatures];
. . .
```

If you refer to the section that explains how naive Bayes works, you'll recall that to compute a probability, you need two so-called partials, one for each dependent variable value. A partial is the product of conditional probabilities and one unconditional probability. For example, to compute the probability of liberal given barista and female, and medium, one partial is the product of P(barista | liberal), P(female | liberal), P(medium | liberal), and P(liberal).

In the demo, for just one partial, you need three conditional probabilities, one for each combination of the specified feature values and the dependent value. But to compute any probability for a binary classification problem, you need both partials corresponding to the two possible dependent variable values. Therefore, if there are two dependent variable values, and three features, you need 2 * 3 = 6 conditional probabilities to compute both partials.

The conditional probabilities are stored in the local matrix conditionals. The row index is the index of the dependent variable, and the column index is the index of the feature value. For example, conditionals[0][2] corresponds to dependent variable 0 (conservative) and feature 2 (income). Put another way, for the demo, the first row of conditionals holds the three conditional probabilities for conservative, and the second row holds the three conditional probabilities for liberal.

Next, array unconditionals, which holds the unconditional probabilities of each dependent variable value, is allocated, and the independent x-values and dependent y-value are converted from strings to integers:

```
double[] unconditionals = new double[2];
int y = this.stringToInt[numFeatures][yValue];
int[] x = new int[numFeatures];
for (int i = 0; i < numFeatures; ++i)
{
  string s = xValues[i];
  x[i] = this.stringToInt[i][s];
}
```

Because a variable representing the number of features is used so often in the code, a design alternative is to create a class member named something like numFeatures, rather than recreate it as a local variable for each method.

Next, the conditional probabilities are computed and stored using count information that was computed by the Train method:

```
for (int k = 0; k < 2; ++k) // each y-value
{
  for (int i = 0; i < numFeatures; ++i)
  {
    int attIndex = i;
    int valIndex = x[i];
    int depIndex = k;
    conditionals[k][i] = (jointCounts[attIndex][valIndex][depIndex] * 1.0) /
      dependentCounts[depIndex];
  }
}
```

Although the code here is quite short, it is some of the trickiest code I've ever worked with when implementing machine learning algorithms. For me at least, sketching out diagrams like those in Figures **4-b** and **4-c** is absolutely essential in order to write the code in the first place, and correct bugs later.

Next, method Probability computes the probabilities of each dependent value and stores those values:

```
int totalDependent = 0; // ex: count(conservative) + count(liberal)
for (int k = 0; k < 2; ++k)
  totalDependent += this.dependentCounts[k];

for (int k = 0; k < 2; ++k)
  unconditionals[k] = (dependentCounts[k] * 1.0) / totalDependent;
```

Notice that I qualify the first reference to member array dependentCounts using the this keyword, but I don't use this on the second reference. From a style perspective, I sometimes use this technique just to remind myself that an array, variable, or object is a class member.

Next, the partials are computed and stored:

```
double[] partials = new double[2];
for (int k = 0; k < 2; ++k)
{
  partials[k] = 1.0; // because we are multiplying
  for (int i = 0; i < numFeatures; ++i)
    partials[k] *= conditionals[k][i];
  partials[k] *= unconditionals[k];
}
```

Next, the sum of the two (for binary classification) partials is computed and stored, and the requested probability is computed and returned:

```
. . .
  double evidence = 0.0;
  for (int k = 0; k < 2; ++k)
    evidence += partials[k];

  return partials[y] / evidence;
}
```

Recall that the sum of partials is sometimes called the evidence term in naive Bayes terminology. Let me reiterate that the code for method probability is very tricky. The key to understanding this code, and many other machine learning algorithms, is having a clear picture (literally) of the data structures, arrays, and matrices used.

Method Accuracy

Method Accuracy computes how well the trained model predicts the dependent variable for a set of training data, or test data, which has known dependent variable values. The accuracy of the model on the training data gives you a rough idea of whether the model is effective or not. The accuracy of the model on the test data gives you a rough estimate of how well the model will predict when presented with new data, where the dependent variable value is not known.

The definition of method Accuracy begins:

```
public double Accuracy(string[][] data)
{
  int numCorrect = 0;
  int numWrong = 0;

  int numRows = data.Length;
  int numCols = data[0].Length;
. . .
```

Next, the method iterates through each data item and extracts the x-values—for example, "barista", "female", and "medium"—and extracts the known y-value—for example, "conservative". The x-values and the y-value are fed to the Probability method. If the computed probability is greater than 0.5, the model has made a correct classification:

```
. . .
  for (int i = 0; i < numRows; ++i) // row
  {
    string yValue = data[i][numCols - 1]; // assumes y in last column
    string[] xValues = new string[numCols - 1];
    Array.Copy(data[i], xValues, numCols - 1);
    double p = this.Probability(yValue, xValues);
    if (p > 0.50)
      ++numCorrect;
    else
      ++numWrong;
  }
  return (numCorrect * 1.0) / (numCorrect + numWrong);
}
```

A common design alternative is to use a different threshold value instead of the 0.5 used here. For example, suppose that for some data item, method Probability returns 0.5001. The classification is just barely correct in some sense. So you might want to count probabilities greater than 0.60 as correct, probabilities of less than 0.40 as wrong, and probabilities between 0.40 and 0.60 as inconclusive.

Converting Numeric Data to Categorical Data

Naive Bayes classification works with categorical data such as low, medium, and high for annual income, rather than numeric values such as $36,000.00. If a data set contains some numeric data and you want to apply naive Bayes classification, one approach is to convert the numeric values to categorical values. This process is called data discretization, or more informally, binning the data.

There are three main ways to bin data. The simplest, called equal width, is to create intervals, or "buckets," of the same size. The second approach, used with equal frequency, is to create buckets so that each bucket has an (approximately) equal number of data values in it. The third approach is to create buckets using a clustering algorithm such as k-means, so that data values are grouped by similarity to each other.

Each of the three techniques has significant pros and cons, so there is no one clear best way to bin data. That said, equal-width binning is usually the default technique.

There are many different ways to implement equal-width binning. Suppose you want to convert the following 10 numeric values to either "small", "medium", "large", or "extra-large" (four buckets) using equal-width binning:

2.0, 3.0, 4.0, 5.0, 6.0, 8.0, 9.0, 10.0, 12.0, 14.0

Here, the data is sorted, but equal-width binning does not require this. First, the minimum and maximum values are determined:

min = 2.0
max = 14.0

Next, the width of each bucket is computed:

width = (max - min) / number-buckets
    = (14.0 - 2.0) / 4
    = 3.0

Next, a preliminary set of intervals that define each bucket are constructed:

```
[2.0, 5.0)  [5.0, 8.0)  [8.0, 11.0)  [11.0, 14.0)  -> interval data
  [0]  [1]    [2] [3]     [4] [5]       [6]  [7]    -> cell index
    {0}          {1}         {2}           {3}       -> bucket
```

Here, the notation [2.0, 5.0) means greater than or equal to 2.0, and also less than 5.0. Next, the two interval end points are modified to capture any outliers that may appear later:

```
[-inf, 5.0)  [5.0, 8.0)  [8.0, 11.0)  [11.0, +inf)  -> interval data
  [0]  [1]     [2] [3]     [4] [5]       [6]  [7]    -> cell index
     {0}          {1}         {2}           {3}       -> bucket
```

Here, -inf and +inf stand for negative infinity and positive infinity. Now the interval data can be used to determine the categorical equivalent of a numeric value. Value 8.0 belongs to bucket 2, so 8.0 maps to "large". If some new data arrives later, it can be binned too. For example, if some new value $x = 12.5$ appears, it belongs to bucket 3 and would map to "extra-large".

One possible implementation of equal-width binning can take the form of two methods: the first to create the interval data, and a second to assign a bucket or category to a data item. For example, a method to create interval data could begin as:

```
static double[] MakeIntervals(double[] data, int numBins) // bin numeric data
{
  double max = data[0]; // find min & max
  double min = data[0];
  for (int i = 0; i < data.Length; ++i)
  {
    if (data[i] < min) min = data[i];
    if (data[i] > max) max = data[i];
  }
  double width = (max - min) / numBins;
. . .
```

Static method MakeIntervals accepts an array of data to bin, and the number of buckets to create, and returns the interval data in an array. The minimum and maximum values are determined, and the bucket width is computed as described earlier.

Next, the preliminary intervals are created:

```
double[] intervals = new double[numBins * 2];
intervals[0] = min;
intervals[1] = min + width;
for (int i = 2; i < intervals.Length - 1; i += 2)
```

```
{
  intervals[i] = intervals[i - 1];
  intervals[i + 1] = intervals[i] + width;
}
```

Notice that when using the scheme described here, all the interval boundary values, except the first and last, are duplicated. It would be possible to store each boundary value just once. Duplicating boundary values may be mildly inefficient, but leads to code that is much easier to understand and modify.

And now, the first and last boundary values are modified so that the final interval data will be able to handle any possible input value:

```
. . .
  intervals[0] = double.MinValue; // outliers
  intervals[intervals.Length - 1] = double.MaxValue;

  return intervals;
}
```

With this binning design, a partner method to perform the binning can be defined:

```
static int Bin(double x, double[] intervals)
{
  for (int i = 0; i < intervals.Length - 1; i += 2)
  {
    if (x >= intervals[i] && x < intervals[i + 1])
      return i / 2;
  }
  return -1; // error
}
```

Static method Bin does a simple linear search until it finds the correct interval. A design alternative is to do a binary search. Calling the binning methods could resemble:

```
double[] data = new double[] { 2.0, 3.0, . . , 14.0 };
double[] intervals = MakeIntervals(data, 4); // 4 bins
int bin = Bin(x, 9.5); // bucket for value 9.5
```

Comments

When presented with a machine learning classification problem, naive Bayes classification is often used first to establish baseline results. The idea is that the assumption of independence of predictor variables is almost certainly not true, so other, more sophisticated classification techniques should create models that are at least as good as a naive Bayes model.

One important area in which naive Bayes classifiers are often used is text and document classification. For example, suppose you want to classify email messages from customers into low, medium, or high priority. The predictor variables would be each possible word in the messages. Naive Bayes classification is surprisingly effective for this type of problem.

Chapter 4 Complete Demo Program Source Code

```
using System;
using System.Collections.Generic;
namespace NaiveBayes
{
  class BayesProgram
  {
    static void Main(string[] args)
    {
      Console.WriteLine("\nBegin Naive Bayes classification demo");
      Console.WriteLine("Goal is to predict (liberal/conservative) from job, " +
        "sex and income\n");

      string[][] rawData = new string[30][];
      rawData[0] = new string[] { "analyst", "male", "high", "conservative" };
      rawData[1] = new string[] { "barista", "female", "low", "liberal" };
      rawData[2] = new string[] { "cook", "male", "medium", "conservative" };
      rawData[3] = new string[] { "doctor", "female", "medium", "conservative" };
      rawData[4] = new string[] { "analyst", "female", "low", "liberal" };
      rawData[5] = new string[] { "doctor", "male", "medium", "conservative" };
      rawData[6] = new string[] { "analyst", "male", "medium", "conservative" };
      rawData[7] = new string[] { "cook", "female", "low", "liberal" };
      rawData[8] = new string[] { "doctor", "female", "medium", "liberal" };
      rawData[9] = new string[] { "cook", "female", "low", "liberal" };
      rawData[10] = new string[] { "doctor", "male", "medium", "conservative" };
      rawData[11] = new string[] { "cook", "female", "high", "liberal" };
      rawData[12] = new string[] { "barista", "female", "medium", "liberal" };
      rawData[13] = new string[] { "analyst", "male", "low", "liberal" };
      rawData[14] = new string[] { "doctor", "female", "high", "conservative" };

      rawData[15] = new string[] { "barista", "female", "medium", "conservative" };
      rawData[16] = new string[] { "doctor", "male", "medium", "conservative" };
      rawData[17] = new string[] { "barista", "male", "high", "conservative" };
      rawData[18] = new string[] { "doctor", "female", "medium", "liberal" };
      rawData[19] = new string[] { "analyst", "male", "low", "liberal" };
      rawData[20] = new string[] { "doctor", "male", "medium", "conservative" };
      rawData[21] = new string[] { "cook", "male", "medium", "conservative" };
      rawData[22] = new string[] { "doctor", "female", "high", "conservative" };
      rawData[23] = new string[] { "analyst", "male", "high", "conservative" };
      rawData[24] = new string[] { "barista", "female", "medium", "liberal" };
      rawData[25] = new string[] { "doctor", "male", "medium", "conservative" };
      rawData[26] = new string[] { "analyst", "female", "medium", "conservative" };
      rawData[27] = new string[] { "analyst", "male", "medium", "conservative" };
      rawData[28] = new string[] { "doctor", "female", "medium", "liberal" };
      rawData[29] = new string[] { "barista", "male", "medium", "conservative" };

      Console.WriteLine("The raw data is: \n");
      ShowData(rawData, 5, true);

      Console.WriteLine("Splitting data into 80%-20% train and test sets");
      string[][] trainData;
      string[][] testData;
      MakeTrainTest(rawData, 15, out trainData, out testData); // seed = 15 is nice
      Console.WriteLine("Done \n");

      Console.WriteLine("Training data: \n");
      ShowData(trainData, 5, true);
```

```
Console.WriteLine("Test data: \n");
ShowData(testData, 5, true);

Console.WriteLine("Creating Naive Bayes classifier object");
Console.WriteLine("Training classifier using training data");
BayesClassifier bc = new BayesClassifier();
bc.Train(trainData); // compute key count data structures
Console.WriteLine("Done \n");

double trainAccuracy = bc.Accuracy(trainData);
Console.WriteLine("Accuracy of model on train data = " +
  trainAccuracy.ToString("F4"));
double testAccuracy = bc.Accuracy(testData);
Console.WriteLine("Accuracy of model on test data  = " +
  testAccuracy.ToString("F4"));

Console.WriteLine("\nPredicting politics for job = barista, sex = female, "
  + "income = medium \n");
string[] features = new string[] { "barista", "female", "medium" };

string liberal = "liberal";
double pLiberal = bc.Probability(liberal, features);
Console.WriteLine("Probability of liberal   = " +
  pLiberal.ToString("F4"));

string conservative = "conservative";
double pConservative = bc.Probability(conservative, features);
Console.WriteLine("Probability of conservative = " +
  pConservative.ToString("F4"));

Console.WriteLine("\nEnd Naive Bayes classification demo\n");
Console.ReadLine();
} // Main

static void MakeTrainTest(string[][] allData, int seed,
  out string[][] trainData, out string[][] testData)
{
  Random rnd = new Random(seed);
  int totRows = allData.Length;
  int numTrainRows = (int)(totRows * 0.80);
  int numTestRows = totRows - numTrainRows;
  trainData = new string[numTrainRows][];
  testData = new string[numTestRows][];

  string[][] copy = new string[allData.Length][]; // ref copy of all data
  for (int i = 0; i < copy.Length; ++i)
    copy[i] = allData[i];

  for (int i = 0; i < copy.Length; ++i) // scramble order
  {
    int r = rnd.Next(i, copy.Length);
    string[] tmp = copy[r];
    copy[r] = copy[i];
    copy[i] = tmp;
  }
  for (int i = 0; i < numTrainRows; ++i)
    trainData[i] = copy[i];
```

```
    for (int i = 0; i < numTestRows; ++i)
      testData[i] = copy[i + numTrainRows];
  } // MakeTrainTest

  static void ShowData(string[][] rawData, int numRows, bool indices)
  {
    for (int i = 0; i < numRows; ++i)
    {
      if (indices == true)
        Console.Write("[" + i.ToString().PadLeft(2) + "]  ");
      for (int j = 0; j < rawData[i].Length; ++j)
      {
        string s = rawData[i][j];
        Console.Write(s.PadLeft(14) + " ");
      }
      Console.WriteLine("");
    }
    if (numRows != rawData.Length-1)
      Console.WriteLine(". . .");
    int lastRow = rawData.Length - 1;
    if (indices == true)
      Console.Write("[" + lastRow.ToString().PadLeft(2) + "]  ");
    for (int j = 0; j < rawData[lastRow].Length; ++j)
    {
      string s = rawData[lastRow][j];
      Console.Write(s.PadLeft(14) + " ");
    }
    Console.WriteLine("\n");
  }

  static double[] MakeIntervals(double[] data, int numBins) // bin numeric data
  {
    double max = data[0]; // find min & max
    double min = data[0];
    for (int i = 0; i < data.Length; ++i)
    {
      if (data[i] < min) min = data[i];
      if (data[i] > max) max = data[i];
    }
    double width = (max - min) / numBins; // compute width

    double[] intervals = new double[numBins * 2]; // intervals
    intervals[0] = min;
    intervals[1] = min + width;
    for (int i = 2; i < intervals.Length - 1; i += 2)
    {
      intervals[i] = intervals[i - 1];
      intervals[i + 1] = intervals[i] + width;
    }
    intervals[0] = double.MinValue; // outliers
    intervals[intervals.Length - 1] = double.MaxValue;

    return intervals;
  }

  static int Bin(double x, double[] intervals)
  {
    for (int i = 0; i < intervals.Length - 1; i += 2)
    {
      if (x >= intervals[i] && x < intervals[i + 1])
```

```
      return i / 2;
    }
    return -1; // error
  }

} // Program

public class BayesClassifier
{
  private Dictionary<string, int>[] stringToInt; // "male" -> 0, etc.
  private int[][][] jointCounts; // [feature][value][dependent]
  private int[] dependentCounts;

  public BayesClassifier()
  {
    this.stringToInt = null; // need training data to know size
    this.jointCounts = null; //  need training data to know size
    this.dependentCounts = null; //   need training data to know size
  }

  public void Train(string[][] trainData)
  {
    // 1. scan training data and construct one dictionary per column
    int numRows = trainData.Length;
    int numCols = trainData[0].Length;
    this.stringToInt = new Dictionary<string, int>[numCols]; // allocate array

    for (int col = 0; col < numCols; ++col) // including y-values
    {
      stringToInt[col] = new Dictionary<string, int>(); // instantiate Dictionary

      int idx = 0;
      for (int row = 0; row < numRows; ++row) // each row of curr column
      {
        string s = trainData[row][col];
        if (stringToInt[col].ContainsKey(s) == false) // first time seen
        {
          stringToInt[col].Add(s, idx); // ex: analyst -> 0
          ++idx;
        }
      } // each row
    } // each col

    // 2. scan and count using stringToInt Dictionary
    this.jointCounts = new int[numCols - 1][][]; // do not include the y-value

    // a. allocate second dim
    for (int c = 0; c < numCols - 1; ++c) // each feature column but not y-column
    {
      int count = this.stringToInt[c].Count; // number possible values for column
      jointCounts[c] = new int[count][];
    }

    // b. allocate last dimension = always 2 for binary classification
    for (int i = 0; i < jointCounts.Length; ++i)
      for (int j = 0; j < jointCounts[i].Length; ++j)
      {
        //int numDependent = stringToInt[stringToInt.Length - 1].Count;
        //jointCounts[i][j] = new int[numDependent];
```

```
      jointCounts[i][j] = new int[2]; // binary classification
    }

    // c. init joint counts with 1 for Laplacian smoothing
    for (int i = 0; i < jointCounts.Length; ++i)
      for (int j = 0; j < jointCounts[i].Length; ++j)
        for (int k = 0; k < jointCounts[i][j].Length; ++k)
          jointCounts[i][j][k] = 1;

    // d. compute joint counts
    for (int i = 0; i < numRows; ++i)
    {
      string yString = trainData[i][numCols - 1]; // dependent value
      int depIndex = stringToInt[numCols - 1][yString]; // corresponding index
      for (int j = 0; j < numCols - 1; ++j)
      {
        int attIndex = j;
        string xString = trainData[i][j]; // an attribute value like "male"
        int valIndex = stringToInt[j][xString]; // corresponding integer like 0
        ++jointCounts[attIndex][valIndex][depIndex];
      }
    }

    // 3. scan and count number of each of the 2 dependent values
    this.dependentCounts = new int[2]; // binary

    for (int i = 0; i < dependentCounts.Length; ++i) // Laplacian init
      dependentCounts[i] = numCols - 1; // numCols - 1 = num features

    for (int i = 0; i < trainData.Length; ++i)
    {
      string yString = trainData[i][numCols - 1]; // conservative or liberal
      int yIndex = stringToInt[numCols - 1][yString]; // 0 or 1
      ++dependentCounts[yIndex];
    }

    return; // the trained 'model' is jointCounts and dependentCounts
  } // Train

  public double Probability(string yValue, string[] xValues)
  {
    int numFeatures = xValues.Length; // ex: 3 (job, sex, income)

    double[][] conditionals = new double[2][]; // binary
    for (int i = 0; i < 2; ++i)
      conditionals[i] = new double[numFeatures]; // ex: P('doctor' | conservative)

    double[] unconditionals = new double[2]; // ex: P('conservative'), P('liberal')

    // convert strings to ints
    int y = this.stringToInt[numFeatures][yValue];
    int[] x = new int[numFeatures];
    for (int i = 0; i < numFeatures; ++i)
    {
      string s = xValues[i];
      x[i] = this.stringToInt[i][s];
    }
```

```
// compute conditionals
for (int k = 0; k < 2; ++k) // each y-value
{
  for (int i = 0; i < numFeatures; ++i)
  {
    int attIndex = i;
    int valIndex = x[i];
    int depIndex = k;
    conditionals[k][i] =
      (jointCounts[attIndex][valIndex][depIndex] * 1.0) /
        dependentCounts[depIndex];
  }
}

// compute unconditionals
int totalDependent = 0; // ex: count(conservative) + count(liberal)
for (int k = 0; k < 2; ++k)
  totalDependent += this.dependentCounts[k];

for (int k = 0; k < 2; ++k)
  unconditionals[k] = (dependentCounts[k] * 1.0) / totalDependent;

// compute partials
double[] partials = new double[2];
for (int k = 0; k < 2; ++k)
{
  partials[k] = 1.0; // because we are multiplying
  for (int i = 0; i < numFeatures; ++i)
    partials[k] *= conditionals[k][i];
  partials[k] *= unconditionals[k];
}

// evidence = sum of partials
double evidence = 0.0;
for (int k = 0; k < 2; ++k)
  evidence += partials[k];

return partials[y] / evidence;
} // Probability

public double Accuracy(string[][] data)
{
  int numCorrect = 0;
  int numWrong = 0;

  int numRows = data.Length;
  int numCols = data[0].Length;

  for (int i = 0; i < numRows; ++i) // row
  {
    string yValue = data[i][numCols - 1]; // assumes y in last column
    string[] xValues = new string[numCols - 1];
    Array.Copy(data[i], xValues, numCols - 1);
    double p = this.Probability(yValue, xValues);
    if (p > 0.50)
      ++numCorrect;
    else
      ++numWrong;
  }
```

```
        return (numCorrect * 1.0) / (numCorrect + numWrong);
    }
} // class BayesClassifier

} // ns
```

Chapter 5 Neural Network Classification

Introduction

Neural networks are software systems that loosely model biological neurons and synapses. Neural network classification is one of the most interesting and sophisticated topics in all of machine learning. One way to think of a neural network is as a complex mathematical function that accepts one or more numeric inputs and generates one or more numeric outputs.

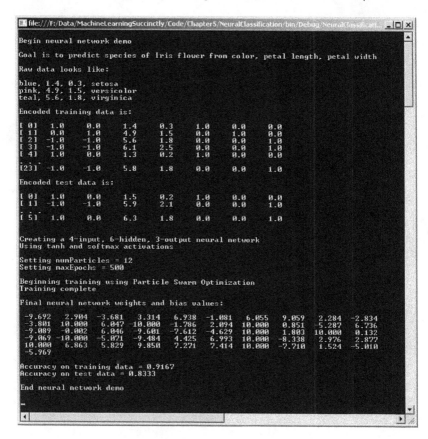

Figure 5-a: Neural Network Classification Demo

A good way to get an understanding of what neural networks are is to examine the screenshot of a demo program in **Figure 5-a**. The goal of the demo is to create a model that can predict the species of an iris flower based on the flower's color, petal length, and petal width.

The source data set has 30 items. The first three data items are:

```
blue, 1.4, 0.3, setosa
pink, 4.9, 1.5, versicolor
teal, 5.6, 1.8, virginica
```

The predictor variables (also called independent variables, features, and x-data) are in the first three columns. The first column holds the iris flower's color, which can be blue, pink, or teal. The second and third columns are the flower's petal length and width. The fourth column holds the dependent variable, species, which can be *setosa*, *versicolor*, or *virginica*.

Note: the demo data is an artificial data set patterned after a famous, real data set called Fisher's Iris data. Fisher's real data set has 150 items and uses sepal length and sepal width instead of color. (A sepal is a green, leaf-like structure).

Because neural networks work internally with numeric data, the categorical color values and species must be encoded as numeric values. The demo assumes this has been done externally. The first three lines of encoded data are:

```
[ 0]   1.0     0.0     1.4     0.3     1.0     0.0     0.0
[ 1]   0.0     1.0     4.9     1.5     0.0     1.0     0.0
[ 2]  -1.0    -1.0     5.6     1.8     0.0     0.0     1.0
```

The species values are encoded using what is called 1-of-N dummy encoding. Categorical data value *setosa* maps to numeric values (1, 0, 0), *versicolor* maps to (0, 1, 0), and *virginica* maps to (0, 0, 1). There are several other, less common, encoding schemes for categorical dependent variables.

The independent variable color values are encoded using 1-of-(N-1) effects encoding. Color blue maps to (1, 0), pink maps to (0, 1), and teal maps to (-1, -1). Although there are alternatives, in my opinion the somewhat unusual looking 1-of-(N-1) effects encoding is usually the best approach to use for categorical predictor variables.

Using the 30-item source data, the demo program sets up a 24-item training set, used to create the neural network model, and a 6-item test set, used to estimate the accuracy of the model when presented with new, previously unseen data.

The demo program creates a four-input-node, six-hidden-node, three-output-node neural network. The number of input and output nodes, four and three, are determined by the structure of the encoded data. The number of hidden nodes for a neural network is a free parameter and must be determined by trial and error.

There are dozens of variations of neural networks. The demo program uses the most basic form, which is a fully-connected, feed-forward architecture, with a hyperbolic tangent (often abbreviated tanh) hidden layer activation function and a softmax output layer activation function. Activation functions will be explained shortly.

Behind the scenes, a 4-6-3 neural network has a total of (4)(6) + 6 + (6)(3) + 3 = 51 numeric values, called weights and biases. These weights determine the output values for a given set of input values. Training a neural network is the process of finding the best set of values for the weights and biases, so that when presented with the training data, the computed outputs closely match the known outputs. Then, when presented with new data, the neural network uses the best weights found to make predictions.

There are several techniques that can be used to train a neural network. By far, the most common technique is called back-propagation. In fact, back-propagation training is so common that people new to neural networks sometimes assume it is the only training technique. The demo program uses an alternative technique called particle swarm optimization (PSO).

Basic PSO training requires just two parameter values. The demo program uses 12 particles, and sets a maximum training loop count of 500. These parameters will be explained shortly.

After the neural network is trained using PSO, the demo program displays the values of the 51 weights and biases that define the model. The demo computes the accuracy of the final model on the training data, which is 91.67% (22 out of 24 correct), and the accuracy on the test data (83.33%, five out of six correct). The 83.33% figure can be interpreted as a rough estimate of how well the final neural network model would predict the species of new, previously unseen iris flowers.

Understanding Neural Network Classification

The process by which a neural network computes output values is called the feed-forward mechanism. Output values are determined by the input values, the hidden weights and bias values, and two activation functions. The process is best explained with a concrete example. See the diagram in **Figure 5-b**.

The diagram shows a fully connected 3-4-2 dummy neural network, which does not correspond to the demo problem. Although the neural network appears to have three layers of nodes, the first layer, the input layer, is normally not counted, so the neural network in the diagram is usually called a two-layer network.

Each arrow connecting one node to another represents a weight value. Each hidden and output node also has an arrow that represents a special weight called a bias. The neural network's three input values are { 1.0, 5.0, 9.0 }, and the two output values are { 0.4886, 0.5114 }.

The feed-forward process begins by computing the values for the hidden nodes. Each hidden node value is an activation function applied to the sum of the products of input node values and their associated weight values, plus the node's bias value. For example, the top-most hidden node's value is computed as:

hidden[0] sum = (1.0)(0.01) + (5.0)(0.05) + (9.0)(0.09) + 0.13
              = 0.01 + 0.25 + 0.81 + 0.13
              = 1.20

hidden[0] value = tanh(1.20)
                = 0.8337 (rounded)

The dummy neural network is using tanh, the hyperbolic tangent function. The tanh function accepts any real value and returns a result that is between -1.0 and +1.0. The main alternative to the tanh function for hidden layer activation is the logistic sigmoid function.

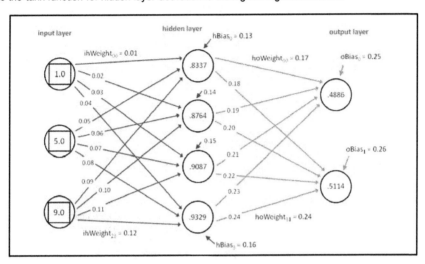

Figure 5-b: The Neural Network Feed-Forward Mechanism

Next, each output node is computed in a similar way. Preliminary output values for all nodes are computed, and then the preliminary values are combined, so that all output node values sum to 1.0. In **Figure 5-b**, the two output node preliminary output values are:

output[0] prelim = (.8337)(.17) + (.8764)(.19) + (.9087)(.21) + (.9329)(.23) + .25
$\qquad$ = 0.9636

output[1] prelim = (.8337)(.18) + (.8764)(.20) + (.9087)(.22) + (.9329)(.24) + .26
$\qquad$ = 1.0091

These two preliminary output values are combined using an activation function called the softmax function to give the final output values like so:

output[0] = $e^{0.9636}$ / ($e^{0.9636}$ + $e^{1.0091}$)
$\qquad$ = 2.6211 / (2.6211 + 2.7431)
$\qquad$ = 0.4886

output[1] = $e^{1.0091}$ / ($e^{0.9636}$ + $e^{1.0091}$)
$\qquad$ = 2.7431 / (2.6211 + 2.7431)
$\qquad$ = 0.5114

The point of using the softmax activation function is to coerce output values to sum to 1.0 so that they can be interpreted as the probabilities of the y-values.

For the dummy neural network in **Figure 5-b**, there are two output nodes, so suppose those nodes correspond to predicting male or female, where male is dummy-encoded as (1, 0) and female is encoded as (0, 1). If the output values (0.4886, 0.5114) are interpreted as probabilities, the higher probability is in the second position, and so the output values predict (0, 1), which is female.

Binary neural network classification, where there are two output values, is a special case that can, and usually is, treated differently from problems with three or more output values. With just two possible y-values, instead of using softmax activation with two output nodes and dummy encoding, you can use the logistic sigmoid function with just a single output node and 0-1 encoding.

The logistic sigmoid function is defined as $f(z) = 1.0 / (1.0 + e^{-z})$. It accepts any real-valued input and returns a value between 0.0 and 1.0. So if two categorical y-values are male and female, you would encode male as 0 and female as 1. You would create a neural network with just one output node. When computing the value of the single output node, you'd use the logistic sigmoid function for activation. The result will be between 0.0 and 1.0, for example, 0.6775. In this case, the computed output, 0.6775, is closer to 1 (female) than to 0 (male) so you'd conclude the output is female.

Another very common design alternative applies to any type of neural network classifier. Instead of using separate, distinct bias values for each hidden and output node, you can consider the bias values as special weights that have a hidden, dummy, constant associated input value of 1.0. In my opinion, treating bias values as special weights with invisible 1.0 inputs is conceptually unappealing, and more error-prone than just treating bias values as bias values.

Demo Program Overall Structure

To create the demo, I launched Visual Studio and selected the new C# console application template. After the template code loaded into the editor, I removed all `using` statements at the top of the source code, except for the single reference to the top-level System namespace. In the Solution Explorer window, I renamed file Program.cs to the more descriptive NeuralProgram.cs, and Visual Studio automatically renamed class Program to NeuralProgram.

The overall structure of the demo program, with a few minor edits to save space, is presented in **Listing 5-a**. In order to keep the size of the example code small, and the main ideas as clear as possible, the demo program omits normal error checking.

```
using System;
namespace NeuralClassification
{
  class NeuralProgram
  {
    static void Main(string[] args)
    {
      Console.WriteLine("Begin neural network demo");
      Console.WriteLine("Goal is to predict species of Iris flower");
      Console.WriteLine("Raw data looks like: ");
      Console.WriteLine("blue, 1.4, 0.3, setosa");
      Console.WriteLine("pink, 4.9, 1.5, versicolor");
      Console.WriteLine("teal, 5.6, 1.8, virginica \n");
```

```
        double[][] trainData = new double[24][];
        trainData[0] = new double[] { 1, 0, 1.4, 0.3, 1, 0, 0 };
        trainData[1] = new double[] { 0, 1, 4.9, 1.5, 0, 1, 0 };
        // etc.
        trainData[23] = new double[] { -1, -1, 5.8, 1.8, 0, 0, 1 };

        double[][] testData = new double[6][];
        testData[0] = new double[] { 1, 0, 1.5, 0.2, 1, 0, 0 };
        testData[1] = new double[] { -1, -1, 5.9, 2.1, 0, 0, 1 };
        // etc.
        testData[5] = new double[] { 1, 0, 6.3, 1.8, 0, 0, 1 };

        Console.WriteLine("Encoded training data is: ");
        ShowData(trainData, 5, 1, true);

        Console.WriteLine("Encoded test data is: ");
        ShowData(testData, 2, 1, true);

        Console.WriteLine("Creating a 4-input, 6-hidden, 3-output neural network");
        Console.WriteLine("Using tanh and softmax activations");
        const int numInput = 4;
        const int numHidden = 6;
        const int numOutput = 3;
        NeuralNetwork nn = new NeuralNetwork(numInput, numHidden, numOutput);

        int numParticles = 12;
        int maxEpochs = 500;
        Console.WriteLine("Setting numParticles = " + numParticles);
        Console.WriteLine("Setting maxEpochs = " + maxEpochs);

        Console.WriteLine("Beginning training using Particle Swarm Optimization");
        double[] bestWeights = nn.Train(trainData, numParticles,
          maxEpochs, exitError, probDeath);
        Console.WriteLine("Final neural network weights and bias values: ");
        ShowVector(bestWeights, 10, 3, true);

        nn.SetWeights(bestWeights);
        double trainAcc = nn.Accuracy(trainData);
        Console.WriteLine("Accuracy on training data = " + trainAcc.ToString("F4"));

        double testAcc = nn.Accuracy(testData);
        Console.WriteLine("Accuracy on test data = " + testAcc.ToString("F4"));

        Console.WriteLine("End neural network demo\n");
        Console.ReadLine();
      } // Main

      static void ShowVector(double[] vector, int valsPerRow, int decimals,
        bool newLine) { . . }

      static void ShowData(double[][] data, int numRows, int decimals,
        bool indices) { . . }

    } // Program class

    public class NeuralNetwork { . . }
  } // ns
```

Listing 5-a: Neural Network Classification Demo Program Structure

All the neural network classification logic is contained in a single program-defined class named NeuralNetwork. All the program logic is contained in the Main method. The Main method begins by setting up 24 hard-coded (color, length, width, species) data items in an array-of-arrays style matrix:

```
static void Main(string[] args)
{
  Console.WriteLine("\nBegin neural network demo\n");
  Console.WriteLine("Raw data looks like: \n");
  Console.WriteLine("blue, 1.4, 0.3, setosa");
  Console.WriteLine("pink, 4.9, 1.5, versicolor");
  Console.WriteLine("teal, 5.6, 1.8, virginica \n");
  double[][] trainData = new double[24][];
  trainData[0] = new double[] { 1, 0, 1.4, 0.3, 1, 0, 0 };
  trainData[1] = new double[] { 0, 1, 4.9, 1.5, 0, 1, 0 };
  trainData[2] = new double[] { -1, -1, 5.6, 1.8, 0, 0, 1 };
. . .
```

The demo program assumes that the color values, blue, pink, and teal, have been converted either manually or programmatically to 1-of-(N-1) encoded form, and that the three species values have been converted to 1-of-N encoded form.

For simplicity, the demo does not normalize the numeric petal length and width values. This is acceptable here only because their magnitudes, all between 0.2 and 7.0, are close enough to the -1, 0, and +1 values of the 1-of-(N-1) encoded color values such that neither feature will dominate the other. In most situations, you should normalize your data.

Next, the demo creates six hard-coded test data items:

```
double[][] testData = new double[6][];
testData[0] = new double[] { 1, 0, 1.5, 0.2, 1, 0, 0 };
testData[1] = new double[] { -1, -1, 5.9, 2.1, 0, 0, 1 };
testData[2] = new double[] { 0, 1, 1.4, 0.2, 1, 0, 0 };
testData[3] = new double[] { 0, 1, 4.7, 1.6, 0, 1, 0 };
testData[4] = new double[] { 1, 0, 4.6, 1.3, 0, 1, 0 };
testData[5] = new double[] { 1, 0, 6.3, 1.8, 0, 0, 1 };
```

In a non-demo scenario, the training and test data would be programmatically generated from the source data set using a utility method named something like MakeTrainTest or SplitData.

After displaying a few lines of the training and test data using static helper method ShowData, the demo program creates and instantiates a program-defined NeuralNetwork classifier object:

```
Console.WriteLine("\nCreating a 4-input, 6-hidden, 3-output neural network");
Console.WriteLine("Using tanh and softmax activations \n");
int numInput = 4;
int numHidden = 6;
int numOutput = 3;
NeuralNetwork nn = new NeuralNetwork(numInput, numHidden, numOutput);
```

There are four input nodes to accommodate two values for the 1-of-(*N*-1) encoded color, plus the petal length and width. There are three output nodes to accommodate the 1-of-*N* encoded three species values: *setosa*, *versicolor*, and *virginica*. Determining the number of hidden nodes to use is basically a matter of trial and error.

Next, the neural network is trained:

```
int numParticles = 12;
int maxEpochs = 500;
Console.WriteLine("Setting numParticles = " + numParticles);
Console.WriteLine("Setting maxEpochs = " + maxEpochs);
Console.WriteLine("\nBeginning training using Particle Swarm Optimization");
double[] bestWeights = nn.Train(trainData, numParticles, maxEpochs);

Console.WriteLine("Training complete \n");
Console.WriteLine("Final neural network weights and bias values:");
ShowVector(bestWeights, 10, 3, true);
```

The demo program uses particle swarm optimization (PSO) for training. There are many variations of PSO, but the demo uses the simplest form, which requires only the number of virtual particles and the maximum number of iterations for the main optimization loop.

After training completes, the best weights found are stored in the NeuralNetwork object. For convenience, the training method also explicitly returns the best weights found. The 51 weights and bias values are displayed using helper method ShowVector. The demo program does not save the weight values that define the model, so you might want to write a SaveWeights method.

The demo program concludes by computing the classification accuracy of the final model:

```
. . .
  nn.SetWeights(bestWeights);
  double trainAcc = nn.Accuracy(trainData);
  Console.WriteLine("\nAccuracy on training data = " + trainAcc.ToString("F4"));

  double testAcc = nn.Accuracy(testData);
  Console.WriteLine("Accuracy on test data = " + testAcc.ToString("F4"));

  Console.WriteLine("\nEnd neural network demo\n");
  Console.ReadLine();
} // Main
```

Note that because the best weights found are stored in the NeuralNetwork object, the call to method SetWeights is not really necessary.

The demo program does not use the model to make a prediction for a new data item that has an unknown species. Prediction could look like:

```
double[] unknown = new double[] { 1, 0, 1.9, 0.5 }; // blue, petal = 1.9, 0.5
nn.SetWeights(bestWeights);
string species = nn.Predict(unknown);
Console.WriteLine("Predicted species is " + species);
```

Defining the NeuralNetwork Class

The structure of the program-defined NeuralNetwork class is presented in **Listing 5-b**. Data member array inputs holds the x-values. Member matrix ihWeights holds the input-to-hidden weights. For example, if ihWeights[0][2] is 0.234, then the weight connecting input node 0 to hidden node 2 has value 0.234.

```
public class NeuralNetwork
{
  private int numInput;   // number of input nodes
  private int numHidden;  // number of hidden nodes
  private int numOutput;  // number of output nodes

  private double[] inputs;
  private double[][] ihWeights; // input-hidden
  private double[] hBiases;
  private double[] hOutputs;

  private double[][] hoWeights; // hidden-output
  private double[] oBiases;
  private double[] outputs;

  private Random rnd;

  public NeuralNetwork(int numInput, int numHidden, int numOutput) { . . }
  private static double[][] MakeMatrix(int rows, int cols)

  public void SetWeights(double[] weights) { . . }

  public double[] ComputeOutputs(double[] xValues) { . . }
  private static double HyperTan(double x) { . . }
  private static double[] Softmax(double[] oSums) { . . }

  public double[] Train(double[][] trainData, int numParticles, int maxEpochs) { . . }
  private void Shuffle(int[] sequence) { . . }
  private double MeanSquaredError(double[][] trainData, double[] weights) { . . }

  public double Accuracy(double[][] testData) { . . }
  private static int MaxIndex(double[] vector) { . . }

  // ------------------------------------------------
  private class Particle { . . }
  // ------------------------------------------------
}
```

Listing 5-b: The NeuralNetwork Class

Member array hBiases holds the hidden node bias values. Member array hOutputs holds the values of the hidden nodes after the hidden layer tanh function has been applied. After they're computed, these values act as local inputs when computing the output layer nodes.

Member matrix hoWeights holds the hidden-to-output node weights. Member array oBiases holds the bias values for the output nodes. Member array outputs holds the final output node values. Member rnd is a Random object, which is used during the PSO training algorithm.

The NeuralNetwork class has a single constructor. Static helper method MakeMatrix is called by the constructor, and is just a convenience to allocate the ihWeights and hoWeights matrices. The constructor code is simple:

```
public NeuralNetwork(int numInput, int numHidden, int numOutput)
{
    this.numInput = numInput;
    this.numHidden = numHidden;
    this.numOutput = numOutput;
    this.inputs = new double[numInput];
    this.ihWeights = MakeMatrix(numInput, numHidden);
    this.hBiases = new double[numHidden];
    this.hOutputs = new double[numHidden];
    this.hoWeights = MakeMatrix(numHidden, numOutput);
    this.oBiases = new double[numOutput];
    this.outputs = new double[numOutput];
    this.rnd = new Random(0);
}
```

Random object rnd is instantiated with a seed value of 0 only because that value gave a representative demo run. You might want to experiment with different seed values.

Method ComputeOutputs implements the feed-forward mechanism. The definition begins:

```
public double[] ComputeOutputs(double[] xValues)
{
    double[] hSums = new double[numHidden]; // hidden nodes sums scratch array
    double[] oSums = new double[numOutput]; // output nodes sums
    . . .
```

Recall that hidden and output nodes are computed in two steps. First, a sum of products is computed, and then an activation function is applied. Arrays hSums and oSums hold the sum of products. A design alternative is to declare hSums and oSums as class-scope arrays to avoid allocating them on every call to ComputeOutputs. However, if you do this, you'd have to remember to explicitly zero out both arrays inside ComputeOutputs.

Next, ComputeOutputs transfers the x-data parameter values into the class inputs array:

```
for (int i = 0; i < xValues.Length; ++i) // copy x-values to inputs
    this.inputs[i] = xValues[i];
```

A very important design alternative is to delete the class inputs array from the NeuralNetwork definition and use the x-data values directly. This saves the overhead of copying values into inputs at the expense of clarity.

Next, the hidden node values are computed using the feed-forward mechanism:

```
for (int j = 0; j < numHidden; ++j)  // sum of weights * inputs
    for (int i = 0; i < numInput; ++i)
        hSums[j] += this.inputs[i] * this.ihWeights[i][j]; // note +=

for (int i = 0; i < numHidden; ++i)  // add biases
    hSums[i] += this.hBiases[i];
```

```
for (int i = 0; i < numHidden; ++i)    // apply activation
  this.hOutputs[i] = HyperTan(hSums[i]);
```

Here, the hyperbolic tangent function is hard-coded into the class definition. A design alternative is to pass the hidden layer activation function in as a parameter. This gives additional calling flexibility at the expense of significantly increased design complexity.

Helper method HyperTan is defined:

```
private static double HyperTan(double x)
{
  if (x < -20.0)
    return -1.0; // approximation is correct to 30 decimals
  else if (x > 20.0)
    return 1.0;
  else return Math.Tanh(x);
}
```

Although you can just call built-in method Math.Tanh directly, the demo checks the input value x first because for small or large values of x, the tanh function returns values that are extremely close to 0.0 or 1.0, respectively.

After computing the hidden node values, method ComputeOutputs computes the output layer node values:

```
for (int j = 0; j < numOutput; ++j)    // sum of weights * hOutputs
  for (int i = 0; i < numHidden; ++i)
    oSums[j] += hOutputs[i] * hoWeights[i][j];

for (int i = 0; i < numOutput; ++i)  // add biases to input-to-hidden sums
  oSums[i] += oBiases[i];

double[] softOut = Softmax(oSums); // all outputs at once for efficiency
Array.Copy(softOut, outputs, softOut.Length);
```

Calculating the softmax outputs is a bit subtle. If you refer to the explanation of how softmax works, you'll notice that the calculation requires all the preliminary outputs, so unlike hidden nodes which are activated one at a time, output nodes are activated as a group.

The definition of helper method Softmax is:

```
private static double[] Softmax(double[] oSums)
{
  // determine max output-sum
  double max = oSums[0];
  for (int i = 0; i < oSums.Length; ++i)
    if (oSums[i] > max) max = oSums[i];

  // determine scaling factor -- sum of exp(each val - max)
  double scale = 0.0;
  for (int i = 0; i < oSums.Length; ++i)
    scale += Math.Exp(oSums[i] - max);
```

```
double[] result = new double[oSums.Length];
for (int i = 0; i < oSums.Length; ++i)
  result[i] = Math.Exp(oSums[i] - max) / scale;

return result; // now scaled so that xi sum to 1.0
}
```

Method Softmax is short, but quite tricky. Instead of computing softmax outputs using the direct definition, method Softmax uses some clever math. The indirect implementation gives the same result as the definition, but avoids potential arithmetic underflow or overflow problems, because intermediate values in the direct-definition calculation can be extremely close 0.0.

Understanding Particle Swarm Optimization

The most common technique to train neural networks is called back-propagation. Back-propagation is based on classical calculus techniques, and is conceptually complex, but relatively simple to implement. The major disadvantage of back-propagation is that it requires you to specify values for two parameters called the learning rate and the momentum. Back-propagation is extraordinarily sensitive to these parameter values, meaning that even a tiny change can have a dramatic impact.

Particle swarm optimization (PSO) also requires parameter values, but is much less sensitive than back-propagation. The major disadvantage of using PSO for training is that it is usually slower than using back-propagation.

PSO is loosely modeled on coordinated group behavior, such as the flocking of birds. PSO maintains a collection of virtual particles where each particle represents a potential best solution to a problem, which, in the case of neural networks, is a set of values for the weights and biases that minimize the error between computed output values and known output values in a set of training data.

Expressed in very high-level pseudo-code, PSO looks like:

```
initialize n particles to random solutions/positions and velocities
loop until done
  for each particle
    compute a new velocity based on best known positions
    use new velocity to move particle to new position/solution
  end for
end loop
return best solution/position found by any particle
```

PSO is illustrated in **Figure 5-c**. In a simple case where a solution consists of two values, like (1.23, 4.56), you can think of a solution as a point on an (x, y) plane. The graph shows two particles. In most situations, there would be many particles. The goal is to minimize the function $f(x, y) = 3x^2 + 3y^2$. The solution is x = y = 0.0, so the problem doesn't really need PSO; the example is intended just to illustrate how PSO works.

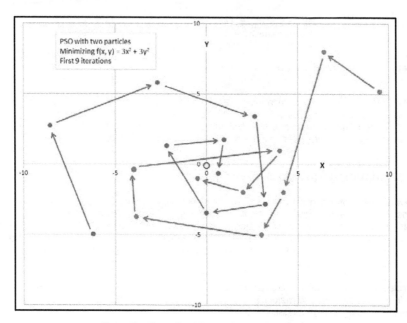

Figure 5-c: Example of Particle Swarm Optimization

The first particle, in the lower left, starts with a randomly generated initial solution of (-6.0, -5.0) and random initial velocity (direction) values that move the particle up and to the left. The second particle, in the upper right, has random initial value (9.5, 5.1) and random initial velocity that will move the particle up and to the left.

The graph shows how each particle moves during the first nine iterations of the main PSO loop. The new position of each particle is influenced by its current direction, the best position found by the particle at any time, and the best position found by any of the particles at any time. The net result is that particles tend to move in a coordinated way and converge on a good, hopefully optimum, solution. In the graph, you can see that both particles quickly got very close to the optimal solution of (0, 0).

In math terms, the PSO equations to update a particle's velocity and position are:

$$v(t+1) = (w * v(t)) + (c1 * r1 * (p(t) − x(t)) + (c2 * r2 * (g(t) − x(t))$$

$$x(t+1) = x(t) + v(t+1)$$

The position update process is actually much simpler than these equations appear. The first equation updates a particle's velocity. The term $v(t+1)$ means the velocity at time t+1. Notice that v is bold, indicating that velocity is a vector value and has multiple components, such as (1.55, -0.33), rather than being a single scalar value.

The new velocity depends on three terms. The first term is $w * v(t)$. The w factor is called the inertia weight and is just a constant like 0.73 (more on this shortly), and $v(t)$ is the current velocity at time t. The second term is $c1 * r1 * (p(t) - x(t))$. The c1 factor is a constant called the cognitive (or personal) weight. The r1 factor is a random variable in the range [0, 1), which is greater than or equal to 0 and strictly less than 1. The $p(t)$ vector value is the particle's best position found so far. The $x(t)$ vector value is the particle's current position.

The third term in the velocity update equation is $(c2 * r2 * (g(t) - x(t)))$. The c2 factor is a constant called the social (or global) weight. The r2 factor is a random variable in the range [0, 1). The $g(t)$ vector value is the best known position found by any particle in the swarm so far. Once the new velocity, $v(t+1)$, has been determined, it is used to compute the new particle position $x(t+1)$.

A concrete example will help make the update process clear. Suppose that you are trying to minimize $f(x, y) = 3x^2 + 3y^2$. Suppose a particle's current position, $x(t)$, is $(x, y) = (3.0, 4.0)$, and that the particle's current velocity, $v(t)$, is (-1.0, -1.5). Additionally, assume that constant $w = 0.7$, constant $c1 = 1.4$, constant $c2 = 1.4$, and that random numbers r1 and r2 are 0.5 and 0.6 respectively. Finally, suppose that the particle's current best known position is $p(t) = (2.5, 3.6)$ and that the current global best known position found by any particle in the swarm is $g(t) = (2.3, 3.4)$. Then the new velocity values are:

$v(t+1) = (0.7 * (-1.0, -1.5)) + (1.4 * 0.5 * (2.5, 3.6) - (3.0, 4.0)) + (1.4 * 0.6 * (2.3, 3.4) - (3.0, 4.0))$
$= (-0.70, -1.05) + (-0.35, -0.28) + (-0.59, -0.50)$
$= (-1.64, -1.83)$

Now the new velocity is added to the current position to give the particle's new position:

$x(t+1) = (3.0, 4.0) + (-1.64, -1.83)$
$= (1.36, 2.17)$

Recall that the optimal solution is $(x, y) = (0, 0)$. Observe that the update process has improved the old position or solution from (3.0, 4.0) to (1.36, 2.17). If you examine the update process, you'll see that the new velocity is the old velocity (times a weight) plus a factor that depends on a particle's best known position, plus another factor that depends on the best known position from all particles in the swarm. Therefore, a particle's new position tends to move toward a better position based on the particle's best known position and the best known position from all particles.

Training using PSO

The implementation of method Train begins:

```
public double[] Train(double[][] trainData, int numParticles, int maxEpochs)
{
    int numWeights = (this.numInput * this.numHidden) + this.numHidden +
      (this.numHidden * this.numOutput) + this.numOutput;
. . .
```

Method Train assumes that the training data has the dependent variable being predicted, iris flower species in the case of the demo, stored in the last column of matrix trainData. Next, relevant local variables are set up:

```
int epoch = 0;
double minX = -10.0; // for each weight
double maxX = 10.0;
double w = 0.729; // inertia weight
double c1 = 1.49445; // cognitive weight
double c2 = 1.49445; // social weight
double r1, r2; // cognitive and social randomizations
```

Variable epoch is the main loop counter variable. Variables minX and maxX set limits for each weight and bias value. Setting limits in this way is called weight restriction. In general, you should use weight restriction only with x-data that has been normalized, or where the magnitudes are all roughly between -10.0 and +10.0.

Variable w, called the inertia weight, holds a value that influences the extent a particle will keep moving in its current direction. Variables c1 and c2 hold values that determine the influence of a particle's best known position, and the best known position of any particle in the swarm. The values of w, c1, and c2 used here are ones recommended by research.

Next, the swarm is created:

```
Particle[] swarm = new Particle[numParticles];
double[] bestGlobalPosition = new double[numWeights];
double bestGlobalError = double.MaxValue;
```

The definition of class Particle is presented in **Listing 5-c**.

```
private class Particle
{
    public double[] position; // equivalent to NN weights
    public double error; // measure of fitness
    public double[] velocity;

    public double[] bestPosition; // best position found so far by this Particle
    public double bestError;

    public Particle(double[] position, double error, double[] velocity,
        double[] bestPosition, double bestError)
    {
        this.position = new double[position.Length];
        position.CopyTo(this.position, 0);
        this.error = error;
        this.velocity = new double[velocity.Length];
        velocity.CopyTo(this.velocity, 0);
        this.bestPosition = new double[bestPosition.Length];
        bestPosition.CopyTo(this.bestPosition, 0);
        this.bestError = bestError;
    }
}
```

Listing 5-c: Particle Class Definition

Class Particle is a container class that holds a virtual position, velocity, and error associated with the position. A minor design alternative is to use a structure instead of a class. The demo program defines class Particle inside class NeuralNetwork. If you refactor the demo code to another programming language that does not support nested classes, you'll have to define class Particle as a standalone class.

Method Train initializes the swarm of particles with his code:

```
for (int i = 0; i < swarm.Length; ++i)
{
  double[] randomPosition = new double[numWeights];
  for (int j = 0; j < randomPosition.Length; ++j)
    randomPosition[j] = (maxX - minX) * rnd.NextDouble() + minX;

  double error = MeanSquaredError(trainData, randomPosition);
  double[] randomVelocity = new double[numWeights];

  for (int j = 0; j < randomVelocity.Length; ++j)
  {
    double lo = 0.1 * minX;
    double hi = 0.1 * maxX;
    randomVelocity[j] = (hi - lo) * rnd.NextDouble() + lo;
  }
  swarm[i] = new Particle(randomPosition, error, randomVelocity,
    randomPosition, error);

  // does current Particle have global best position/solution?
  if (swarm[i].error < bestGlobalError)
  {
    bestGlobalError = swarm[i].error;
    swarm[i].position.CopyTo(bestGlobalPosition, 0);
  }
}
```

There's quite a lot going on here, and so you may want to refactor the code into a method named something like InitializeSwarm. For each particle, a random position is generated, subject to the minX and maxX constraints. The random position is fed to helper method MeanSquaredError to determine the associated error. A significant design alternative is to use a different form of error called the mean cross entropy error.

Because a particle velocity consists of values that are added to the particle's current position, initial random velocity values are set to be smaller (on average, one-tenth) than initial position values. The 0.1 scaling factor is to a large extent arbitrary, but has worked well in practice.

After a random position and velocity have been created, those values are fed to the Particle constructor. The call to the constructor may look a bit odd at first glance. The last two arguments represent the particle's best position found and the error associated with that position. So, at particle initialization, these best-values are the initial position and error values.

After initializing the swarm, method Train begins the main loop, which uses PSO to seek a set of best weights:

```
int[] sequence = new int[numParticles]; // process particles in random order
```

```
for (int i = 0; i < sequence.Length; ++i)
  sequence[i] = i;

while (epoch < maxEpochs)
{
  double[] newVelocity = new double[numWeights];
  double[] newPosition = new double[numWeights];
  double newError;
  Shuffle(sequence);
  . . .
```

In general, when using PSO it is better to process the virtual particles in random order. Local array sequence holds the indices of the particles and the indices are randomized using a helper method Shuffle, which uses the Fisher-Yates algorithm:

```
private void Shuffle(int[] sequence)
{
  for (int i = 0; i < sequence.Length; ++i)
  {
    int ri = rnd.Next(i, sequence.Length);
    int tmp = sequence[ri];
    sequence[ri] = sequence[i];
    sequence[i] = tmp;
  }
}
```

The main processing loop executes a fixed maxEpochs times. An important alternative is to exit early if the current best error drops below some small value. The code could resemble:

```
if (bestGlobalError < exitError)
  break;
```

Here, exitError would be passed as a parameter to method Train or the Particle constructor. The training method continues by updating each particle. The first step is to compute a new random velocity (speed and direction) based on the current velocity, the particle's best known position, and the swarm's best known position:

```
for (int pi = 0; pi < swarm.Length; ++pi) // each Particle (index)
{
  int i = sequence[pi];
  Particle currP = swarm[i]; // for coding convenience

  for (int j = 0; j < currP.velocity.Length; ++j) // each x-value of the velocity
  {
    r1 = rnd.NextDouble();
    r2 = rnd.NextDouble();

    newVelocity[j] = (w * currP.velocity[j]) +
      (c1 * r1 * (currP.bestPosition[j] - currP.position[j])) +
      (c2 * r2 * (bestGlobalPosition[j] - currP.position[j]));
  }
  newVelocity.CopyTo(currP.velocity, 0);
```

This code is the heart of the PSO algorithm, and it is unlikely you will need to modify it. After a particle's new velocity has been computed, that velocity is used to compute the particle's new position, which represents the neural network's set of weights and bias values:

```
for (int j = 0; j < currP.position.Length; ++j)
{
  newPosition[j] = currP.position[j] + newVelocity[j]; // compute new position
  if (newPosition[j] < minX) // keep in range
    newPosition[j] = minX;
  else if (newPosition[j] > maxX)
    newPosition[j] = maxX;
}
newPosition.CopyTo(currP.position, 0);
```

Notice the new position is constrained by minX and maxX, which is essentially implementing neural network weight restriction. A minor design alternative is to remove this constraining mechanism. After the current particle's new position has been determined, the error associated with that position is computed:

```
newError = MeanSquaredError(trainData, newPosition);
currP.error = newError;
if (newError < currP.bestError) // new particle best?
{
  newPosition.CopyTo(currP.bestPosition, 0);
  currP.bestError = newError;
}

if (newError < bestGlobalError) // new global best?
{
  newPosition.CopyTo(bestGlobalPosition, 0);
  bestGlobalError = newError;
}
```

At this point, method Train has finished processing each particle, and so the main loop counter variable is updated. A significant design addition is to implement code that simulates the death of a particle. The idea is to kill a particle with a small probability, and then give birth to a new particle at a random location. This helps prevent the swarm from getting stuck at a non-optimal solution at the risk of killing a good particle (one that is moving to an optimal solution).

After the main loop finishes, method Train concludes. The best position (weights) found is copied into the neural network's weight and bias matrices and arrays, using class method SetWeights, and these best weights are also explicitly returned:

```
. . .
  SetWeights(bestGlobalPosition); // best position is a set of weights
  double[] retResult = new double[numWeights];
  Array.Copy(bestGlobalPosition, retResult, retResult.Length);
  return retResult;
} // Train
```

Method SetWeights is presented in the complete demo program source code at the end of this chapter. Notice all the weights and bias values are stored in a single array, which corresponds to the best position found by any particle. This means that there is an implied ordering of the weights. The demo program assumes input-to-hidden weights are stored first, followed by hidden node biases, followed by hidden-to-output weights, followed by output node biases.

Other Scenarios

This chapter presents all the key information needed to understand and implement a neural network system. There are many additional, advanced topics you might wish to investigate. The biggest challenge when working with neural networks is avoiding over-fitting. Over-fitting occurs when a neural network is trained so that the resulting model has perfect or near-perfect accuracy on the training data, but the model predicts poorly when presented with new data. Holding out a test data set can help identify when over-fitting has occurred. A closely related technique is called k-fold cross validation. Instead of dividing the source data into two sets, the data is divided into k sets, where k is often 10.

Another approach for dealing with over-fitting is to divide the source data into three sets: a training set, a validation set, and a test set. The neural network is trained using the training data, but during training, the current set of weights and bias values are periodically applied to the validation data. Error on both the training and validation data will generally decrease during training, but when over-fitting starts to occur, error on the validation data will begin to increase, indicating training should stop. Then, the final model is applied to the test data to get a rough estimate of the model's accuracy.

A relatively new technique to deal with over-fitting is called dropout training. As each training item is presented to the neural network, half of the hidden nodes are ignored. This prevents hidden nodes from co-adapting with each other, and results in a robust model that generalizes well. Drop-out training can also be applied to input nodes. A related idea is to add random noise to input values. This is sometimes called jittering.

Neural networks with multiple layers of hidden nodes are often called deep neural networks. In theory, a neural network with a single, hidden layer can solve most classification problems. This is a consequence of what is known as the universal approximation theorem, or sometimes, Cybenko's theorem. However, for some problems, such as speech recognition, deep neural networks can be more effective than ordinary neural networks.

The neural network presented in this chapter measured error using mean squared error. Some research evidence suggests an alternative measure, called cross entropy error, can generate more accurate neural network models. In my opinion, the research supporting the superiority of cross entropy error over mean squared error is fairly convincing, but the improvement gained by using cross entropy error is small. In spite of the apparent superiority of cross entropy error, the use of mean squared error seems to be more common.

Ordinary neural networks are called feed-forward networks because when output values are computed, information flows from input nodes to hidden nodes to output nodes. It is possible to design neural networks where some or all of the hidden nodes have an additional connection that feeds back into themselves. These are called recurrent neural networks.

Chapter 5 Complete Demo Program Source Code

```
using System;
namespace NeuralClassification
{
    class NeuralProgram
    {
        static void Main(string[] args)
        {
            Console.WriteLine("\nBegin neural network demo\n");
            Console.WriteLine("Goal is to predict species from color, petal length, width \n");
            Console.WriteLine("Raw data looks like: \n");
            Console.WriteLine("blue, 1.4, 0.3, setosa");
            Console.WriteLine("pink, 4.9, 1.5, versicolor");
            Console.WriteLine("teal, 5.6, 1.8, virginica \n");

            double[][] trainData = new double[24][];
            trainData[0] = new double[] { 1, 0, 1.4, 0.3, 1, 0, 0 };
            trainData[1] = new double[] { 0, 1, 4.9, 1.5, 0, 1, 0 };
            trainData[2] = new double[] { -1, -1, 5.6, 1.8, 0, 0, 1 };
            trainData[3] = new double[] { -1, -1, 6.1, 2.5, 0, 0, 1 };
            trainData[4] = new double[] { 1, 0, 1.3, 0.2, 1, 0, 0 };
            trainData[5] = new double[] { 0, 1, 1.4, 0.2, 1, 0, 0 };
            trainData[6] = new double[] { 1, 0, 6.6, 2.1, 0, 0, 1 };
            trainData[7] = new double[] { 0, 1, 3.3, 1.0, 0, 1, 0 };
            trainData[8] = new double[] { -1, -1, 1.7, 0.4, 1, 0, 0 };
            trainData[9] = new double[] { 0, 1, 1.5, 0.1, 0, 1, 1 };
            trainData[10] = new double[] { 0, 1, 1.4, 0.2, 1, 0, 0 };
            trainData[11] = new double[] { 0, 1, 4.5, 1.5, 0, 1, 0 };
            trainData[12] = new double[] { 1, 0, 1.4, 0.2, 1, 0, 0 };
            trainData[13] = new double[] { -1, -1, 5.1, 1.9, 0, 0, 1 };
            trainData[14] = new double[] { 1, 0, 6.0, 2.5, 0, 0, 1 };
            trainData[15] = new double[] { 1, 0, 3.9, 1.4, 0, 1, 0 };
            trainData[16] = new double[] { 0, 1, 4.7, 1.4, 0, 1, 0 };
            trainData[17] = new double[] { -1, -1, 4.6, 1.5, 0, 1, 0 };
            trainData[18] = new double[] { -1, -1, 4.5, 1.7, 0, 0, 1 };
            trainData[19] = new double[] { 0, 1, 4.5, 1.3, 0, 1, 0 };
            trainData[20] = new double[] { 1, 0, 1.5, 0.2, 1, 0, 0 };
            trainData[21] = new double[] { 0, 1, 5.8, 2.2, 0, 0, 1 };
            trainData[22] = new double[] { 0, 1, 4.0, 1.3, 0, 1, 0 };
            trainData[23] = new double[] { -1, -1, 5.8, 1.8, 0, 0, 1 };

            double[][] testData = new double[6][];
            testData[0] = new double[] { 1, 0, 1.5, 0.2, 1, 0, 0 };
            testData[1] = new double[] { -1, -1, 5.9, 2.1, 0, 0, 1 };
            testData[2] = new double[] { 0, 1, 1.4, 0.2, 1, 0, 0 };
            testData[3] = new double[] { 0, 1, 4.7, 1.6, 0, 1, 0 };
            testData[4] = new double[] { 1, 0, 4.6, 1.3, 0, 1, 0 };
            testData[5] = new double[] { 1, 0, 6.3, 1.8, 0, 0, 1 };

            Console.WriteLine("Encoded training data is: \n");
            ShowData(trainData, 5, 1, true);

            Console.WriteLine("Encoded test data is: \n");
            ShowData(testData, 2, 1, true);

            Console.WriteLine("\nCreating a 4-input, 6-hidden, 3-output neural network");
            Console.WriteLine("Using tanh and softmax activations \n");
            int numInput = 4;
```

```
      int numHidden = 6;
      int numOutput = 3;
      NeuralNetwork nn = new NeuralNetwork(numInput, numHidden, numOutput);

      int numParticles = 12;
      int maxEpochs = 500;

      Console.WriteLine("Setting numParticles = " + numParticles);
      Console.WriteLine("Setting maxEpochs = " + maxEpochs);

      Console.WriteLine("\nBeginning training using Particle Swarm Optimization");
      double[] bestWeights = nn.Train(trainData, numParticles, maxEpochs);
      Console.WriteLine("Training complete \n");
      Console.WriteLine("Final neural network weights and bias values:");
      ShowVector(bestWeights, 10, 3, true);

      nn.SetWeights(bestWeights);
      double trainAcc = nn.Accuracy(trainData);
      Console.WriteLine("\nAccuracy on training data = " + trainAcc.ToString("F4"));

      double testAcc = nn.Accuracy(testData);
      Console.WriteLine("Accuracy on test data = " + testAcc.ToString("F4"));

      Console.WriteLine("\nEnd neural network demo\n");
      Console.ReadLine();
    } // Main

    static void ShowVector(double[] vector, int valsPerRow, int decimals, bool newLine)
    {
      for (int i = 0; i < vector.Length; ++i)
      {
        if (i % valsPerRow == 0) Console.WriteLine("");
        Console.Write(vector[i].ToString("F" + decimals).PadLeft(decimals + 4) + " ");
      }
      if (newLine == true) Console.WriteLine("");
    }

    static void ShowData(double[][] data, int numRows, int decimals, bool indices)
    {
      for (int i = 0; i < numRows; ++i)
      {
        if (indices == true)
          Console.Write("[" + i.ToString().PadLeft(2) + "]  ");
        for (int j = 0; j < data[i].Length; ++j)
        {
          double v = data[i][j];
          if (v >= 0.0)
            Console.Write(" "); // '+'
          Console.Write(v.ToString("F" + decimals) + "    ");
        }
        Console.WriteLine("");
      }
      Console.WriteLine(". . .");
      int lastRow = data.Length - 1;
      if (indices == true)
        Console.Write("[" + lastRow.ToString().PadLeft(2) + "]  ");
      for (int j = 0; j < data[lastRow].Length; ++j)
      {
        double v = data[lastRow][j];
```

```
      if (v >= 0.0)
        Console.Write(" "); // '+'
      Console.Write(v.ToString("F" + decimals) + "    ");
    }
    Console.WriteLine("\n");
  }
} // Program

public class NeuralNetwork
{
  private int numInput; // number of input nodes
  private int numHidden;
  private int numOutput;

  private double[] inputs;
  private double[][] ihWeights; // input-hidden
  private double[] hBiases;
  private double[] hOutputs;

  private double[][] hoWeights; // hidden-output
  private double[] oBiases;
  private double[] outputs;

  private Random rnd;

  public NeuralNetwork(int numInput, int numHidden, int numOutput)
  {
    this.numInput = numInput;
    this.numHidden = numHidden;
    this.numOutput = numOutput;
    this.inputs = new double[numInput];
    this.ihWeights = MakeMatrix(numInput, numHidden);
    this.hBiases = new double[numHidden];
    this.hOutputs = new double[numHidden];
    this.hoWeights = MakeMatrix(numHidden, numOutput);
    this.oBiases = new double[numOutput];
    this.outputs = new double[numOutput];
    this.rnd = new Random(0);
  } // ctor

  private static double[][] MakeMatrix(int rows, int cols) // helper for ctor
  {
    double[][] result = new double[rows][];
    for (int r = 0; r < result.Length; ++r)
      result[r] = new double[cols];
    return result;
  }

  public void SetWeights(double[] weights)
  {
    // copy weights and biases in weights[] array to i-h weights,
    // i-h biases, h-o weights, h-o biases
    int numWeights = (numInput * numHidden) + (numHidden * numOutput) +
      numHidden + numOutput;
    if (weights.Length != numWeights)
      throw new Exception("Bad weights array length: ");

    int k = 0; // points into weights param

    for (int i = 0; i < numInput; ++i)
```

```
      for (int j = 0; j < numHidden; ++j)
        ihWeights[i][j] = weights[k++];
    for (int i = 0; i < numHidden; ++i)
      hBiases[i] = weights[k++];
    for (int i = 0; i < numHidden; ++i)
      for (int j = 0; j < numOutput; ++j)
        hoWeights[i][j] = weights[k++];
    for (int i = 0; i < numOutput; ++i)
      oBiases[i] = weights[k++];
}

public double[] ComputeOutputs(double[] xValues)
{
    double[] hSums = new double[numHidden]; // hidden nodes sums scratch array
    double[] oSums = new double[numOutput]; // output nodes sums

    for (int i = 0; i < xValues.Length; ++i) // copy x-values to inputs
      this.inputs[i] = xValues[i];

    for (int j = 0; j < numHidden; ++j) // compute i-h sum of weights * inputs
      for (int i = 0; i < numInput; ++i)
        hSums[j] += this.inputs[i] * this.ihWeights[i][j]; // note +=

    for (int i = 0; i < numHidden; ++i) // add biases to input-to-hidden sums
      hSums[i] += this.hBiases[i];

    for (int i = 0; i < numHidden; ++i)   // apply activation
      this.hOutputs[i] = HyperTan(hSums[i]); // hard-coded

    for (int j = 0; j < numOutput; ++j)   // compute h-o sum of weights * hOutputs
      for (int i = 0; i < numHidden; ++i)
        oSums[j] += hOutputs[i] * hoWeights[i][j];

    for (int i = 0; i < numOutput; ++i) // add biases to input-to-hidden sums
      oSums[i] += oBiases[i];

    double[] softOut = Softmax(oSums); // all outputs at once for efficiency
    Array.Copy(softOut, outputs, softOut.Length);

    double[] retResult = new double[numOutput];
    Array.Copy(this.outputs, retResult, retResult.Length);
    return retResult;
}

private static double HyperTan(double x)
{
    if (x < -20.0)
      return -1.0; // approximation is correct to 30 decimals
    else if (x > 20.0)
      return 1.0;
    else
      return Math.Tanh(x);
}

private static double[] Softmax(double[] oSums)
{
    // does all output nodes at once so scale doesn't have to be re-computed each time
    // determine max output-sum
    double max = oSums[0];
```

```
      for (int i = 0; i < oSums.Length; ++i)
        if (oSums[i] > max) max = oSums[i];

      // determine scaling factor -- sum of exp(each val - max)
      double scale = 0.0;
      for (int i = 0; i < oSums.Length; ++i)
        scale += Math.Exp(oSums[i] - max);

      double[] result = new double[oSums.Length];
      for (int i = 0; i < oSums.Length; ++i)
        result[i] = Math.Exp(oSums[i] - max) / scale;

      return result; // now scaled so that xi sum to 1.0
    }

    public double[] Train(double[][] trainData, int numParticles, int maxEpochs)
    {
      int numWeights = (this.numInput * this.numHidden) + this.numHidden +
        (this.numHidden * this.numOutput) + this.numOutput;

      // use PSO to seek best weights
      int epoch = 0;
      double minX = -10.0; // for each weight. assumes data is normalized or 'nice'
      double maxX = 10.0;
      double w = 0.729; // inertia weight
      double c1 = 1.49445; // cognitive weight
      double c2 = 1.49445; // social weight
      double r1, r2; // cognitive and social randomizations

      Particle[] swarm = new Particle[numParticles];
      // best solution found by any particle in the swarm
      double[] bestGlobalPosition = new double[numWeights];
      double bestGlobalError = double.MaxValue; // smaller values better

      // initialize each Particle in the swarm with random positions and velocities
      double lo = 0.1 * minX;
      double hi = 0.1 * maxX;
      for (int i = 0; i < swarm.Length; ++i)
      {
        double[] randomPosition = new double[numWeights];
        for (int j = 0; j < randomPosition.Length; ++j)
          randomPosition[j] = (maxX - minX) * rnd.NextDouble() + minX;

        double error = MeanSquaredError(trainData, randomPosition);
        double[] randomVelocity = new double[numWeights];

        for (int j = 0; j < randomVelocity.Length; ++j)
          randomVelocity[j] = (hi - lo) * rnd.NextDouble() + lo;

        swarm[i] = new Particle(randomPosition, error, randomVelocity,
          randomPosition, error);

        // does current Particle have global best position/solution?
        if (swarm[i].error < bestGlobalError)
        {
          bestGlobalError = swarm[i].error;
          swarm[i].position.CopyTo(bestGlobalPosition, 0);
        }
      }
```

```
// main PSO algorithm
int[] sequence = new int[numParticles]; // process particles in random order
for (int i = 0; i < sequence.Length; ++i)
  sequence[i] = i;

while (epoch < maxEpochs)
{
  double[] newVelocity = new double[numWeights]; // step 1
  double[] newPosition = new double[numWeights]; // step 2
  double newError; // step 3

  Shuffle(sequence); // move particles in random sequence

  for (int pi = 0; pi < swarm.Length; ++pi) // each Particle (index)
  {
    int i = sequence[pi];
    Particle currP = swarm[i]; // for coding convenience

    // 1. compute new velocity
    for (int j = 0; j < currP.velocity.Length; ++j) // each value of the velocity
    {
      r1 = rnd.NextDouble();
      r2 = rnd.NextDouble();

      // velocity depends on old velocity, best position of particle, and
      // best position of any particle
      newVelocity[j] = (w * currP.velocity[j]) +
        (c1 * r1 * (currP.bestPosition[j] - currP.position[j])) +
        (c2 * r2 * (bestGlobalPosition[j] - currP.position[j]));
    }
    newVelocity.CopyTo(currP.velocity, 0);

    // 2. use new velocity to compute new position
    for (int j = 0; j < currP.position.Length; ++j)
    {
      newPosition[j] = currP.position[j] + newVelocity[j];
      if (newPosition[j] < minX) // keep in range
        newPosition[j] = minX;
      else if (newPosition[j] > maxX)
        newPosition[j] = maxX;
    }
    newPosition.CopyTo(currP.position, 0);

    // 3. compute error of new position
    newError = MeanSquaredError(trainData, newPosition);
    currP.error = newError;

    if (newError < currP.bestError) // new particle best?
    {
      newPosition.CopyTo(currP.bestPosition, 0);
      currP.bestError = newError;
    }

    if (newError < bestGlobalError) // new global best?
    {
      newPosition.CopyTo(bestGlobalPosition, 0);
      bestGlobalError = newError;
    }
  } // each Particle
```

```csharp
      ++epoch;
    } // while

    SetWeights(bestGlobalPosition); // best position is a set of weights
    double[] retResult = new double[numWeights];
    Array.Copy(bestGlobalPosition, retResult, retResult.Length);
    return retResult;
  } // Train

  private void Shuffle(int[] sequence)
  {
    for (int i = 0; i < sequence.Length; ++i)
    {
      int ri = rnd.Next(i, sequence.Length);
      int tmp = sequence[ri];
      sequence[ri] = sequence[i];
      sequence[i] = tmp;
    }
  }

  private double MeanSquaredError(double[][] trainData, double[] weights)
  {
    this.SetWeights(weights); // copy the weights to evaluate in

    double[] xValues = new double[numInput]; // inputs
    double[] tValues = new double[numOutput]; // targets
    double sumSquaredError = 0.0;
    for (int i = 0; i < trainData.Length; ++i) // walk through each training item
    {
      // the following assumes data has all x-values first, followed by y-values!
      Array.Copy(trainData[i], xValues, numInput); // extract inputs
      Array.Copy(trainData[i], numInput, tValues, 0, numOutput); // extract targets
      double[] yValues = this.ComputeOutputs(xValues);
      for (int j = 0; j < yValues.Length; ++j)
        sumSquaredError += ((yValues[j] - tValues[j]) * (yValues[j] - tValues[j]));
    }
    return sumSquaredError / trainData.Length;
  }

  public double Accuracy(double[][] testData)
  {
    // percentage correct using winner-takes all
    int numCorrect = 0;
    int numWrong = 0;
    double[] xValues = new double[numInput]; // inputs
    double[] tValues = new double[numOutput]; // targets
    double[] yValues; // computed Y

    for (int i = 0; i < testData.Length; ++i)
    {
      Array.Copy(testData[i], xValues, numInput); // parse test data
      Array.Copy(testData[i], numInput, tValues, 0, numOutput);
      yValues = this.ComputeOutputs(xValues);
      int maxIndex = MaxIndex(yValues); // which cell in yValues has largest value?

      if (tValues[maxIndex] == 1.0) // ugly
        ++numCorrect;
      else
        ++numWrong;
    }
```

```csharp
      return (numCorrect * 1.0) / (numCorrect + numWrong);
    }

    private static int MaxIndex(double[] vector) // helper for Accuracy()
    {
      // index of largest value
      int bigIndex = 0;
      double biggestVal = vector[0];
      for (int i = 0; i < vector.Length; ++i)
      {
        if (vector[i] > biggestVal)
        {
          biggestVal = vector[i];
          bigIndex = i;
        }
      }
      return bigIndex;
    }

    // -----------------------------------------------
    private class Particle
    {
      public double[] position; // equivalent to NN weights
      public double error; // measure of fitness
      public double[] velocity;

      public double[] bestPosition; // best position found by this Particle
      public double bestError;

      public Particle(double[] position, double error, double[] velocity,
        double[] bestPosition, double bestError)
      {
        this.position = new double[position.Length];
        position.CopyTo(this.position, 0);
        this.error = error;
        this.velocity = new double[velocity.Length];
        velocity.CopyTo(this.velocity, 0);
        this.bestPosition = new double[bestPosition.Length];
        bestPosition.CopyTo(this.bestPosition, 0);
        this.bestError = bestError;
      }
    }
    // -----------------------------------------------

  } // NeuralNetwork
} // ns
```

www.ingramcontent.com/pod-product-compliance
Lightning Source LLC
Chambersburg PA
CBHW071251050326
40690CB00011B/2350